He Sets Me On My High Places

Gwynneth Sunshine

O&U
Onwards & Upwards

He Sets Me On My High Places

Onwards and Upwards Publishers
4 The Old Smithy, London Road, Rockbeare,
EX5 2EA, United Kingdom.
www.onwardsandupwards.org

Copyright © Gwynneth Sunshine 2021

The moral right of Gwynneth Sunshine to be identified as the author of this work has been asserted by the author in accordance with the Copyright, Designs and Patents Act 1988.

All rights reserved.

No part of this publication may be reproduced or transmitted in any form or by any means, electronic or mechanical, including photocopy, recording or any information storage and retrieval system, without permission in writing from the author or publisher.

First edition, published in the United Kingdom by Onwards and Upwards Publishers (2021).

ISBN: 978-1-78815-515-1
Typeface: Sabon LT
Graphic design: LM Graphic Design

The views and opinions expressed in this book are the author's own, and do not necessarily represent the views and opinions of Onwards and Upwards Publishers or its staff.

Unless otherwise indicated, scripture quotations are taken from the New King James Version®. Copyright © 1982 by Thomas Nelson. Used by permission. All rights reserved.

Scripture quotations marked (KJV) are from The Authorized (King James) Version. Rights in the Authorized Version in the United Kingdom are vested in the Crown. Reproduced by permission of the Crown's patentee, Cambridge University Press.

Endorsements

The long awaited follow-up to Gwynneth's first book *Darkness to Destiny* takes us on a spiritual journey from a newly saved Christian to spiritual maturity. She perfectly marries the experiences of the new believer on this path with sound scriptural teaching. When travelling this road, we may wonder at times what is actually happening to us, but Gwynneth explains it clearly as part of God's divine plan to bring us into alignment with His perfect will. As she says in her epilogue, "Go God's way, and not your own. The Christian walk does not consist of how much God blesses us, but rather how we may please and bless God and others through a life of obedience to him." I can relate strongly with what Gwynneth teaches in this book.

Keith Brown
Pastor, Southend Full Gospel Church
Southend-on-Sea, Essex

My heart leapt as I started reading this book because I was so encouraged to find clear, simple teaching that is rooted in reality.

Gwynneth draws on her life adventures and experiences to bring insights that are laced with power, passion and practicality.

This book has the potential to change you into the person God meant you to be.

Cleland Thom
Journalist and Author

About the Author

Gwynneth Sunshine is the author of the previously published true story *Darkness to Destiny*. She has a daughter and three grandchildren and lives in Essex, where she attends a local Elim Pentecostal Church. As a Christian she has an evangelistic heart for the marginalised, and for many decades a calling by God to minister to those addicted to drugs and alcohol, to find restoration through a relationship with God. Gwynneth's interests include painting in acrylics, attending an English literature group, writing poetry, and country walks with her dog, and she is a fledgling local artist!

You can find Gwynneth online:

On her website	http://darknesstodestiny.weebly.com
On Facebook	www.facebook.com/Darkness-to-Destiny-631007183764321
On YouTube	www.youtube.com/channel/UCqBygTODtJBsl3nCyiB-WVQ

To my twin sister, Frances Walker:

Your strength in the face of adversity and your unwavering faith and trust in Jesus inspired me to write this book and explore the stages of spiritual growth I have journeyed. Whilst I was writing, the Holy Spirit prompted me to evaluate my Christian walk these past forty-eight years.

You inspire me to walk on the high places with God, standing strong in my faith and trusting Jesus who knows our destiny.

This book is dedicated to you with my love.

Acknowledgements

He Sets Me On My High Places chronicles nearly fifty years of experience as a Christian, as I have journeyed life's highs and lows. My aim is that whilst you read the stages of spiritual growth unravelling in these pages, you may join me and identify with me along the journey, and maybe ponder on your own spiritual growth and relationship with God.

My grateful thanks must go to Pastor Keith Brown of Southend Full Gospel Church, who embraced my autobiography *Darkness to Destiny* and has invited me on numerous occasions to preach in his church and share my testimony. His unwavering support for Darkness to Destiny Ministries and endorsing this, my second book, has been of immense encouragement to me.

My thanks extend to Cleland Thom, author and journalist, in endorsing *He Sets Me On My High Places* and seeing the possibilities within this book to hearten and provoke within the reader a deeper walk and devotion to God.

My acknowledgement would not be complete without my grateful thanks to Luke Jeffery of Onwards and Upwards Publishers, and his team, who took on this second book and worked in a professional manner and with competency.

To my sister, Frances Walker, I thank her for her enthusiasm for this book and its message, which kept me focussed whilst I was writing and editing long hours! I have dedicated *He Sets Me On My High Places* to Frances Walker and acknowledge her as one who has travelled the dark night of the soul with great courage, inspiration and grace.

Lastly, without the Holy Spirit's work in my life and the gentle nudging of the Holy Spirit to write this book, a follow-up to my autobiography *Darkness to Destiny*, it would not have been written. To God I owe my heartfelt thanks, for without travelling these stages of spiritual growth there would be no book. I would not be the person I am today. The glory goes to God.

Contents

Preface 9

1. The Beginnings of a Faith in God 11
2. The False Covering..23
3. The Firm Foundation 34
4. Growing in Christ and the Cost of Discipleship 47
5. The Carnal Nature Wars Against the Spiritual Nature 60
6. Spiritual Warriors 71
7. Living in His Presence 77
8. The Power of the Gift of Tongues..........................89
9. Growing in the Knowledge of God 97
10. The Dark Nights of the Soul and the Spirit 109
11. The Quest for Spiritual Enlightenment................124

Epilogue 134

He Sets Me On My High Places

Preface

I WAS ENCOURAGED BY MATURE CHRISTIANS TO WRITE A teaching book to clarify some of the experiences I went through in my autobiography *Darkness to Destiny*. The result is this teaching book, *He Sets Me On My High Places*, based on the Bible and God's spiritual outworking in my life over the past decades.

Several themes emerged whilst writing which I have presented as stages of spiritual growth along with my personal experience with God. It is a journey where God has corrected, sanctified, and guided me in my Christian walk. These stages of spiritual development align with biblical doctrine and truth.

This is a teaching book, yet my purpose in writing is not for it to become another theological book stacked on a bookshelf!

My endeavour is to present an honest account of biblical truth as I understand it, with the input of my thoughts and experiences, and also inserted within these pages are people's accounts of their spiritual experience, written in their own words.

I have attempted to present the Bible in a format the reader can relate to. I believe those new in the Christian faith and the Christian community at large require effective discipleship on themes such as dying to self, the flesh warring against the spirit, spiritual warfare, the baptism in the Holy Spirit, spiritual gifts, and the dark night of the soul. My aim is for the reader to glean a new insight into their spiritual walk with God as they read this book.

God's wisdom is required to understand Bible truths and for this truth to enrich our spirits. Equally, a lack of divine revelation and knowledge will undoubtedly hinder spiritual growth. "My people are destroyed for lack of knowledge, because you have rejected knowledge." (Hos.4:6).

In conclusion, my intention is not to point the finger in judgement, but rather to acknowledge that all Christians have their trials and temptations. We are in it together! Which of us has not wrestled with doubts and questions about our faith? None of us are alone or unique in this.

Our quest ought to be, "I press toward the goal for the prize of the upward call of God in Christ Jesus." (Phil.3:14).

"Therefore, my beloved, as you have always obeyed, not as in my presence only, but now much more in my absence, work out your own salvation with fear and trembling; for God it is who works in you both to will and to do for His good pleasure." (Phil.2:12,13).

May our aim always be to encourage one another along life's journey.

Chapter One

The Beginnings of a Faith in God

HAVE YOU CONSIDERED 'DANCING WITH THE DEVIL'? IT might seem a strange question to ask, but there is a reason for it. We could argue most people are not particularly spiritually inclined and the notion of 'partying' with the devil is an absurd suggestion. Or we might contend it would not be too absurd if somebody were a practising witch, or even a satanist possessing occult powers! It would appear feasible to dance with the devil then, wouldn't it?

We ought to firstly pose the question, does the devil exist? Cartoon images of the devil in newspaper articles and magazines present a grotesque caricature of an entity with horns, grasping a long-pronged fork! One could hardly take this image of the devil seriously.

If you are a Bible-believing Christian, you will most probably believe in the authenticity of the devil's existence, according to the Bible. As a committed Christian you would not dare to dally in the devil's territory, would you? Not intentionally anyway!

A while ago a Christian proposed to me, "It's fine dallying in the devil's territory occasionally and having a bit of fun!"

This comment took me aback and inwardly I admitted to questioning this person's commitment to God, on how such an ambiguous statement as this could possibly be right for a Christian to live his life by. The liberal idea presented to me, was that it was acceptable for Christians to dip their toes into the devil's arena and out again at whim! I was not expecting to hear these words from a Christian, and up until this point in our conversation there was no indication of such a view.

One could respond by saying to those who enjoy dallying in Satan's territory, "Does it matter what people believe or how they act anyway?" They have got a point, haven't they?

When answering those who partake in occult practices, one could validate such practices by explaining along these lines: "God is a crutch for weak-minded people who pray for help from God through tough times. It is none of our business whether someone worships the devil or God, and it should not matter. It is their life and they are free to choose how they live."

How many of us have concluded that it is only possible to believe in what we can touch, hear, see, and smell? The existence of God cannot be proved, can it?

My thoughts on this subject were similar before I became a 'born again' Christian. The Bible speaks of Nicodemus, a religious ruler of the day, who, when he was presented with the truth of the 'born again' experience, was challenged on his religious beliefs.

Hasn't this happened in our lives too? At some point we are presented with 'truths' which challenge our opinions or traditions on God and His existence as Creator. We imagine how the world was formed. We are often adamant in our beliefs and stick rigidly to them.

On the other hand, maybe we do not believe in any superior being or spirit. "I am an atheist," people adamantly claim and then someone comes along and puts a spanner in the works and shares their 'born again' experience, according to John chapter 3.

"There it is again!" we exclaim. "Another viewpoint, and an unordinary account of a person's experience of God's existence!" We become confused and question our belief system – and just when we thought our set of beliefs were so strong!

Dennis and Rita Bennett explain in their book, *The Holy Spirit and You*, the born-again experience is one where God created mankind for the intention of "responding to God" and having a relationship with God, within "the very inmost part" of a man which is "our spirit, or pneuma in Greek".[1]

Is Religion the Answer?

Let me share with you my early experience on religion. I believed that praying outside of a church building was unnecessary, in the context of adding purpose in my teenage life. It never crossed my mind that God was interested in me!

I had decided early on in my young life there was no place in the world for religion, which caused wars, and I quickly came to the

---

[1] Dennis and Rita Bennett; *The Holy Spirit and You;* p.14.

conclusion that religion could not provide a conclusive answer to the world's problems. The influence of religion on dividing communities was regularly documented in the media and on television. In my younger years I was swayed by the media and the information I absorbed whilst reading and listening to current affairs.

Boarding school was home for me for five years. I attended a vocational school which majored in ballet. The pupils were prompt in their attendance at the local Anglo Catholic church. We were forced to rise early on Sunday mornings and walk up the hill to church.

I resented church life because of these early morning trips in the cold and the arduous routine of walking up the hill in all weathers. Once inside the church we recited the creed and listened to 'sermons' on politics about the dire state of the world! I surmised politics must have a great deal to do with religion.

I wondered much on this connection between politics and religion and would have liked an answer to another question, that of the devil's existence. I imagined the devil as a figment of people's vivid imagination, or maybe a figure from folklore!

Repentance – A Change in Direction

It was many years later when, as a mature Christian, I reflected on the behaviour of a minority of Christians, whose lifestyle appeared no different to unbelievers, despite praying the occasional prayer and never missing church. Had they repented at the Cross of Calvary when it was plain to see their actions did not reflect a holy life? When I thought on their conduct and the hypocrisy of living their Christian life this way, it brought several points to mind.

Firstly, the significance of how Christians introduce the gospel of Christianity to unbelievers and the unchurched – because this will undoubtedly make an impression and influence how they respond to the gospel message.

Secondly, the way we explain the gospel to people has an impact on their actions after they have surrendered their lives to God. Christians should be eager to see a change in the new believer with a desire to live according to biblical principles and commands. If the new believer is discipled well then their conduct will reflect the spiritual new birth with a desire to walk closely with God.

Repentance must precede conversion. The forgiveness of sin follows this act of repentance.[2] The conversion experience requires a heartfelt response to God through repentance. Repentance means making a deliberate decision to leave one's old ways of living behind which are contrary to God's laws of righteousness in the Bible.

The Spirit's Quickening

When a person has insight into religious doctrine but yet is without the Holy Spirit's quickening in knowing the power of the Cross to save them from a Christ-less eternity, without the 'born again' experience, religion amounts to head knowledge and becomes ineffectual and powerless to save the soul.

We have to understand that after we receive Christ as our Lord we become "ministers of a new covenant", we have comprehension that the letter kills, but "the Spirit", the Holy Spirit within the regenerated believer, gives spiritual "life" (2.Cor.3:6).

The new believer has passed from spiritual death into spiritual life. If your head is full of spiritual knowledge it will not save you from hell and an eternity without Christ. The regeneration of the Holy Spirit is essential in saving the soul.

Neil Richardson in his book, *Who on Earth is God?*, in his extract, "Paul and the Problem of Sin", writes that the language of Paul in the Bible "points to the same transforming, liberating experience" which Paul had found.

The apostle Paul elucidates this when he says, "And do not be conformed to this world, but be transformed by the renewing of your mind, that you may prove what is that good and acceptable and perfect will of God." (Rom.12:2).

We can conclude that the conversion experience creates within us a new thinking pattern in following kingdom values.

Neil Richard endorses the apostle Paul's words in Romans 12:2, in saying Paul's experience went further than a mere "intellectual rejuvenation"; in fact, Paul was not alluding to this, for he knew a more profound and lasting change had happened. Paul was aware his experience of renewal had nothing to do with an intellectual response to

---

[2] See Acts 3:19.

biblical doctrine; he knew "a power outside of himself" alone could achieve a change of direction in his life. Oh, how we need this too!

Without this quickening within one's spirit of the living God which the apostle Paul encountered, and the outworking of faith through the Holy Spirit, any change we make in our lifestyle through self-effort will fall far short of God's standard.

The Bible says, "And all our righteousness are like filthy rags." (Is.64:6).

When we are converted, we are aware of a quickening in our spirit. This is the spiritual rebirth. It happens when we repent of our sin and receive a divine revelation of the Cross and its significance on the destiny of our soul and our eternal destination.

We grasp an understanding through the spiritual rebirth experience that the death of Jesus on the Cross was for us as individuals, as opposed to knowing Jesus died for the whole world in an abstract way.

We become recipients of this new, spiritual life. The witness of our spirit with God's Spirit is the evidence that we have been born anew.

The Bible puts it this way: "Therefore, if anyone is in Christ, he is a new creation; old things have passed away; behold all things have become new." (2.Cor.5:17).

If we look at Paul's experience and the evidence of Romans 12:2, it bypasses any idea that intellectual comprehension and one's capability to act righteously could be responsible for Paul's encounter with an Almighty, Holy God.

We are encouraged after we are born again to consciously be filled with the Holy Spirit and our minds renewed by His word, so we may live righteously through the Holy Spirit's indwelling

Understanding the Unchurched

I experienced a change in lifestyle when I asked Jesus to forgive me for my sin. I no longer desired the old ways which I had lived my life by, and which previously dominated my actions before I came to faith in Jesus. I walked by faith, trusting Jesus along this new road. I actively agreed with God to not fight with my peers at school and I stopped using foul expletives. Other lifestyle patterns and habits also needed to change.

From the age of thirteen I was actively engaged as a spiritualist medium. My friend who introduced me to the gospel warned me from the scriptures how my occult practices were contrary to God's commands and would spiritually harm me. I repented of these occult practices before God. It dawned on me that my past involvement in spiritualism was abhorrent to God. I immediately ceased all occult and spiritualism activities after my conversion.

You may appreciate from my past involvement in spiritualism, and living alongside pupils from varying social, spiritual, and economic backgrounds, that our outlook on religion was diverse and derived from our respective cultures.

Whilst putting into perspective my early experiences of religion and spiritualism into the context of that of my fellow pupils, who were influenced by their cultures and countries, we may appreciate the wisdom needed by Christians to understand the different cultures and traditions when engaging with the unchurched. Unbelievers will present the believer with their alternative belief systems.

We should listen to their questions on faith matters, which will vary widely because of their culture and upbringing. We must be watchful of differing perspectives on spiritual matters and of course we should ask God for discernment when conversing with people.

For example, it is quite normal for the unchurched to misunderstand the Bible, having little knowledge or none on the scriptures and the parables. Unbelievers may not have attended Sunday school in the same way as believers who have grown up in church and are familiar with the Bible. It would be beneficial to guard against the tendency of taking biblical knowledge for granted.

Christians require God's wisdom and discernment in deciding if a person is a backslidden Christian, or if they are an unbeliever who is showing an interest in the gospel. It is not unusual for people to be open on matters of faith which they find difficult to express. Have they received the witness of the Spirit? Are they born again? These questions must be asked to get a glimpse of the bigger picture.

When we are born again of the Spirit of God there is no doubt. The Bible says, "The Spirit Himself bears witness with our spirit that we are children of God." (Rom.8:16). In other words, we *know* and are sure we are a Christian.

That Old-fashioned Word, 'Sin'

Sin is an old-fashioned word by today's standards, and rarely used in a world where morals are compromised, yet the word 'sin' is a biblical word which Christians need not be afraid of using when sharing Jesus.

There is a difference between knowing that Jesus died on the Cross to forgive sin through His resurrection from the dead and having a clear understanding that through the death and resurrection of Jesus a way has been made of reconciliation to God and fellowship with Him. We will live with Jesus eternally when we die.[3] The 'born again' experience through the power of the Cross to forgive sin has enabled a way for mankind to pass from spiritual death into life eternal and that journey starts now!

The Bible states we are born sinners and our relationship with God and our fellow men is broken and therefore our ethics are the consequence of these fragmented connections with one another.

Our conscience often lies dormant and does not recognise we have fallen short of God's laws. Instead we make excuses for our failings. The conscience is lulled to sleep. It takes the quickening of the Holy Spirit to reveal the condition of our conscience and our faults.

Through the blood of Jesus shed on the Cross, we may experience a right relationship with God and with others. When our behaviour is contrary to God's word, we may ask Jesus for His forgiveness.

Watchman Nee writes in *The Normal Christian Life* that the blood of Christ is our starting point when we recognise "its value" to "deal with our sin and justifying us in the sight of God".[4]

God establishes a yearning within our soul to know Him. It is this wooing to Himself which creates in us a response to move towards Him. Our spiritual eyes are slowly opened to the implications of the sinless Son of God dying in our place on Calvary.

The punishment for sin should have been ours, yet Jesus was crucified, bleeding, His body disfigured for the wrongs we have committed. This act of Jesus' self-sacrificial death and His crucifixion can transform us into born-again believers, sealed with His Spirit.[5]

---

[3] See Romans 6:23.
[4] Watchman Nee; *The Normal Christian Life;* Chapter 1: The Blood of Christ. See also Romans 3:23.
[5] See John 3:16.

Justified – <u>Just</u> As <u>If</u> <u>I'd</u> Never Sinned

Nothing could save us from hell and sin and justify us, except the blood of Jesus, and thus present us faultless before the Father in Heaven, as if we had never sinned. Jesus is the bridge between our sin and God.

We are justified through the power of the Cross to forgive us of our sin. Jesus looks at us as if we had never sinned when we invite Him into our life.

God speaks about this response from mankind to Jesus as He calls us to Himself: "Behold I stand at the door and knock. If anyone hears My voice and opens the door, I will come into Him and dine with Him, and he with Me." (Rev.3:20).

The Bible elucidates the truth we are justified through faith in Jesus. "Being justified freely by His grace through the redemption that is in Christ Jesus, whom God set forth as a propitiation by His blood through faith, to demonstrate His righteousness, because in His forbearance God had passed over the sins that were previously committed, to demonstrate at the present time His righteousness, that He might be just and the justifier of the one who has faith in Jesus." (Rom.3:24-26).

We are justified before the Father through Jesus' blood shed on Calvary, just as if we had never sinned. The sinless Son of God was innocent, yet it was only He who could take our place by dying for the sins of the whole world and present us faultless before the Father's throne.

Cayhan Osman is a born-again Christian. Here is his account written in his own words on his conversion experience and how Jesus has changed his life.

Cayhan Osman's Testimony of Salvation

I was in and out of prison for years on drug offences and related crimes. I was full of anger and I had a lot of losses from my past which I did not know how to deal with.

I am a British-born Turkish Cypriot. Whilst I was in prison the Muslims made me go to the mosque. If I did not go, they would threaten me with violence, so I decided to go along. It did not make any difference to my life.

I came out of Onley prison in Warwickshire in January 2016 and I had nowhere to go. I came back to North London where I grew up, but I could not go to my dad's because I had caused him enough

The Beginnings of a Faith in God

trouble. I wandered around the streets all night. I had been to the mosque before, but the Iman became angry and impatient with me and told me to come back later.

I found myself in Crouch End, North London one Sunday, where I found myself walking past a small building next to the leisure centre. I heard beautiful singing coming from inside. I hung around and was going to walk past when traffic, including lorries, seemed to sweep me nearer towards the building. Eventually I went inside.

Two women were clearing up after their meeting. It was a small church. I told them my story and that I had nowhere to go. They made me a cup of tea and gave me some food from their church lunch but said they could not help me with accommodation. After they prayed for me, I left.

That week I went to the Council to see if they could find me accommodation. I would not leave until they found me somewhere. They gave me a place in a halfway house in Crouch End, St Mungo's. The next Monday I went back to the church who had helped me and thanked them. I asked if they could pray for me to get a television. They did! On the way home I saw a man loading a television into a van and I asked him if he needed it. He did not and so I had the television.

I went back to the church the following week to say thank you and this time I stayed for the meeting. Roger Forster, the church founder, was there, who had been driven to the meeting by a guy from Chile. We call him Chile Chris.

Chris gave his testimony before Roger preached, on how years ago he had been a drug dealer across Europe. He had met Jesus and was full of life and joy. He invited anyone who wanted to know Jesus to come up and he would pray for them. I did not want to move, but my body took me up there! He led me through a prayer and in front of everyone, I gave my life to Jesus.

I started attending the church regularly. I got a job which was cash in hand. I got my driving licence back and found a flat. I met a woman through my work as a tyre fitter at a garage. I thought, "This is it; I'm made now. God has been good to me." I had everything I wanted, and so I kind of put God into a box and took Him out whenever I needed Him.

I lost everything again. I had everything, but there were things in my life I needed to deal with, and they were coming back to bite me. I had stopped going to church and I ended up on the streets again, doing drugs and homeless.

I went back to the church and one of the women, Sarah, got me into a hostel. I hated it. I came out again. I got myself another job and another flat but once again lost it all. I felt so ashamed.

I'd been visiting other churches in Crouch End and around that area. I went into the Legacy Church in Palmer's Green, where they had talked about addiction and mentioned Teen Challenge ministry. Martyn, the leader, helped me to get in touch with them and they said they had a place for me. In November 2017 I moved to Ilford and into the Teen Challenge centre.

From the moment I joined Teen Challenge I loved it. I felt the Lord everywhere. I knew I was home. I began to speak in tongues and in March 2018 I was baptised. It was tough at times, but I found myself.

Earlier this year in 2019, I went with a team to Holland to a Teen Challenge conference. It was brilliant.

In London, every week we give food to the homeless in Whitechapel; other teams go to four other places in London, to talk to people about Jesus.

I work picking up and delivering furniture to customers, which is a business Teen Challenge runs. I share my testimony with people and pray for them. I have led seven people to the Lord this year.

I am still living in the Teen Challenge house while I get back on my feet. I want to start my own mobile tyre fitting business and move to a home near my church, Ichthus Abide, in Crouch End, where I first came to know Jesus. Life is looking great.

My 'Born Again' Experience

Here is my account of my 'born again' experience.

I recall my reaction to the gospel as a teenager and my response when I heard the gospel of Jesus for the first time.

A school friend animated a glowing presence. This was unusual. I had not noticed this before about my friend. The dramatic change from the loud girl I knew into a compassionate saint, was one I could not understand!

My friend shared her Christian faith with me on what Jesus meant to her and the significance of her faith. Her conversion to Christianity was only the day before she shared with me her new faith in knowing

The Beginnings of a Faith in God

Jesus as her personal Saviour. On reflection it was astonishing, as a new Christian, the eloquence she conveyed in sharing her 'born again' experience with me.

My friend said Jesus could give me a new life! She read from the Bible. I was captivated hearing about Jesus and His words and what He did for people when He walked the earth two thousand years ago. She explained Jesus had died two thousand years ago on the Cross and rose again on the third day from the dead for my sin.

The amazing truth that Jesus died for mankind to deliver them from hell began to have an impact and also that Jesus died for me personally so I could have a relationship with Him on earth, and into eternity![6]

In between school lessons I engaged in occult activity. I had no awareness I was engaging in Satan's territory. I was a depressive character, but my fluctuating moods seemed to stabilise temporarily when I received messages as a spiritualist medium. I did not understand I was being controlled by familiar spirits.

The Bible warns us, "Give no regard to mediums and familiar spirits; do not seek after them, to be defiled by them: I am the Lord your God." (Lev.19:31).

Unbeknown to me then, I was under the influence of evil spirits. I was content to journey through life as a spiritualist. Why would I need Jesus? The friend who introduced me to the Bible, was acutely aware I needed Jesus' forgiveness and His restoring power, and I needed to invite Jesus to come into my life as my Saviour.

One night, five months after my friend first shared Jesus with me, I knelt in my dormitory at boarding school and prayed. This would be the starting point of my Christian journey. I asked Jesus to forgive my sin.

It became clear to me I had been delving in the devil's territory. My spiritual eyes were opened to see my occult involvement. I had participated in contacting evil spirits who masqueraded as messengers from God and now I knew that the occult was abhorrent to God's commands and His laws written in the Bible.

Kneeling on the dormitory floor at night, as a teenager, I repented of my sin. I knew of a certainty that night, inviting Jesus into my life,

---

[6] See John 3:16.

I was His child and Jesus' blood had washed my sin away. I had been born again of the Spirit of God.

Jesus bridged the gulf between God and mankind caused because of our sin and which had separated us from a relationship with God, by His dying on the Cross of Calvary.

This same Jesus is wooing you to Himself to accept His gift of salvation, and He is waiting for your response to His call.

Chapter Two

The False Covering

THE FALSE COVERINGS WE ADOPT TO HIDE FROM THE TRUTH about ourselves and God vary. To appreciate what a false spiritual covering is and its disguises, and the dangers inherent when a Christian unwittingly adopts one, let us first look at the book of Genesis and the creation story. The book of Genesis clearly reveals the nature and origin of the false covering.

We read, "In the beginning, God created the heavens and the earth." (Gen.1:1). God created the light and the darkness; He created the waters "...and let the dry land appear, and it was so. And God called the dry land earth, and the gathering together of the waters he called seas. And God saw that it was good." (Gen.1:9).

God created the grass, "the herb that yields seed, and the fruit tree that yields fruit according to its kind, whose seed is in itself, on the earth; and it was so" (v.11).

"And God blessed them saying, be fruitful and multiply, and fill the waters in the seas, and let birds multiply on the earth." (v.22).

God created the whales in verse 21. He blessed them to be fruitful and to multiply (v.22).

God's creation is unique and is not a duplicate, but the original expression of the characteristics of God. It is therefore fitting for the Hebrew word *bara* meaning 'to create' to be used in this context. The Bible declares in Psalm 146:6 and Acts 17:24 God's sovereignty as Creator of the earth. God's creation is special because it differs from when we make our creation out of a material which is already in existence.

When God made the earth, He made the galaxies and the cosmos, not from something which is already in existence, but out of nothing. "God who gives life to the dead and calls those things which do not exist as though they did." (Rom.4:17).

Russell Grigg explains that there are two attributes of God which atheists undermine and argue against. One is "God's omniscience/omnipotence", the truth that God created "everything right the very first time".[7] The other is the biblical evidence God's creation was "very good" (Gen.1:31). Grigg puts it like this: "...everything God created demonstrated the goodness of God," and furthermore there was no "trial and error" when God created the earth. He explains this contradicts Carl Sagan's view of God being a "sloppy manufacturer", but rather that God's creation in its entirety "demonstrated the goodness of God".

We cannot disarticulate the "claim God created" and neither can scientists "observe it", says Richardson, but by using our biblical knowledge we may investigate it.

God had a desire beyond His creation of the earth, seas, and animals, which was to create mankind in His own image, who would dwell on the earth. Mankind were to have dominion over the animals, the fish, the foul, the cattle, over all the earth (v.26). The earth was to be a place of fruitfulness and blessing. God viewed His handiwork and saw that "it was very good" (Gen.1:31). He desired fellowship with mankind and created the first man, Adam, "a living being", out of the dust to walk upon the earth He had created, in the Garden of Eden (Gen.2:7,8).

God was acting as lawgiver in Genesis 2:17. Grigg explains God commanded Adam "not to eat from the Tree of the Knowledge of Good and Evil in the Garden of Eden".

The Lord made the tree of life also in the midst of the garden.
And the tree of knowledge of good and evil.

Genesis 2:9

There was one thing missing in the garden of Eden and that was a "help meet", a companion for Adam so he would not be alone. God made a woman from the rib of the first man Adam and brought her to him (Gen.2:21,22). The Bible clearly states they were both made in the image of God (Gen.1:26,27).

Grigg explains this union between Adam and Eve is the origin "of the whole human race" and derived "from a single pair" (Gen.3:20). From this union came the doctrine of marriage in Genesis 2:24,25. Jesus confirms the doctrine of marriage in the New Testament (Matt.19:4-6). The marriage union has been created by God between a man and a

---

[7] Russel Grigg; "Genesis the seedbed of all Christian doctrine"; *creation.com*.

woman and not a homosexual relationship between two men or two women, which contravenes God's laws.

We have an insight into the serpent who frequented the garden of Eden and who subtly planted seeds of doubt into the woman's mind. He said to the woman, "Has God indeed said, you shall not eat of every tree of the garden?" (Gen.3:1). Eve, the woman God had created, was oblivious to the serpent's deception. The serpent was skilful in evil, twisting God's words to suit his agenda, in an afront of rebellion towards God's creation where sin would not exist, and mankind and creation would live together in harmony.

God's desire is for a relationship with mankind. He wants us to see Him as more than Creator of the earth. His heart's desire is for us to live in harmony with Him in a loving relationship and on a foundation which is built on our compliance by fully trusting Him.

For God's plan and purpose to prevail, we must recognise that He is sovereign over the creation He created and is the lawgiver of mankind.

God the Lawgiver

We see an explanation and understand God as the lawgiver when God commanded Adam not to eat of a specific tree in the Garden of Eden, "the tree of the knowledge of good and evil" (Gen.2:17).

Creation.com clarifies that God as "the lawgiver" gave Adam a command from His sovereign position as Creator "in exercising His authority in the world". The site goes on further to say that God's sovereignty is "seen in four outstanding events, Creation, The Fall, Choice, Call and Direction of four outstanding people, Abraham, Isaac, Jacob, and Joseph."

The serpent's agenda was in opposition to God as the lawgiver in the Garden of Eden, undermining God's sovereignty. The serpent's subtlety is clear when speaking with half-truths to Eve. She fell for his deception when the serpent's temptation and his plausible words coerced her to eat of the forbidden fruit.

The woman replied to the serpent with God's instructions to her, "We may eat the fruit of the trees of the garden; but of the fruit of the tree, which is in the midst of the garden, God has said, 'You shall not eat it, nor shall you touch it, lest you die.'" (Gen.3:2,3).

Adam and Eve behaved according to God's law in the Garden of Eden, until Eve gave into temptation and tasted of the forbidden fruit, violating God's law. Eve asked Adam to also eat of the fruit and in so doing chose to transgress God's command not to eat the forbidden fruit.

Since the fall of Adam and Eve mankind has had an innate sin nature. "The first sin brought the first guilt."[8]

The serpent lured Eve into a trap by saying it was acceptable to God to eat all the fruit in the garden, yet God had specifically said that they were not to touch the tree in the middle of the garden. The serpent incited the woman with the words, "You shall not surely die." (v.4).

Temptation and Failure – Adopting the False Covering

The devil tempts us to disbelieve God's word. Instead we cover up our faults when we fail God. We forget He forgives us and do not see ourselves in the light of scripture. The schemes of the serpent have not changed since Eve. Satan continues to tempt Christians to doubt the word of God as being absolute and authoritative.

How are we tempted to go astray? One way we are tempted and fall away from God is when we engage in worldly pursuits and our minds are not fixed on God's word about ourselves and our circumstance, even though we are aware the answer to our plight is found in the Bible.

> *But each one is tempted when he is drawn away by his own desires and enticed.*
>
> *James 1:14*

When we give in to temptation we doubt the Bible, and the carnal nature adopts a false covering in an aim to make sense of our circumstances, and because sin separates us from God, we are drawn away from truth when we hide from God and do not acknowledge our backslidden state. Sin has pulled us away from the lawgiver's commands and precepts.

Reckon Yourselves Dead to Sin

The Bible is the place where we should seek knowledge on divine truth. The Bible tells us that we are dead to our sin and alive in God. This means we must understand how God sees and views sin. We should take the same stance over sin in our life as God does, which will empower us, and we will gain victory over it. We must abhor sin as the foul thing it is.

---

[8] *creation.com*

Watchman Nee expands on this point: on facing a dilemma, in reckoning ourselves dead to sin, we then become aware of "something moving inside" our sin nature, appearing very much alive. He explains we face the test of believing the "tangible facts" in the "natural realm"; that is, our sinful nature doesn't seem as dead as we previously thought it to be. Or we embrace the "intangible facts of the spiritual realm which are neither seen nor scientifically proved".[9]

> *Likewise ye also, reckon yourselves to be dead indeed to sin, but alive to God in Christ Jesus our Lord.*
>
> Romans 6:11

Watchman Nee explains that the word 'reckon' relates *only* to the past, in the reckoning ourselves dead to our sin nature. We can count on this as having already happened in the past. He explains that we look back on this divine truth as something already "settled, and not forward yet to be".

By reckoning ourselves dead to sin, when we fall into sin, we can align ourselves spiritually with God's word in agreement. When we sin, we may apply the blood of Jesus to forgive us.

> *If we confess our sins, He is faithful and just to forgive us our sins and to cleanse us from all unrighteousness.*
>
> 1 John 1:9

> *...knowing that our old man was crucified with Him, that the body of sin might be done away with, that we should no longer be slaves of sin.*
>
> Romans 6:6

The latter verse reveals that sin does not have dominion over the Christian. It no longer has the power to control us unless we choose to allow it by engaging in wilful sin.

Becoming Gods in Ourselves

Satan is familiar with the word of God and he will use it deceitfully by twisting God's word to his advantage. The serpent told Adam and Eve they would not die if they ate of the tree in the midst of the garden, but,

---

[9] Watchman Nee; *The Normal Christian Life.*

"...your eyes will be opened, and you will be like God knowing good and evil." (Gen.3:5).

The downfall of mankind occurred in the Garden of Eden when Satan planted the seeds of rebellion into Adam's heart that he could take charge of his life and live independently from God's laws.

God had given Adam and Eve a covering, and the covering was being "created in his own image" (Gen.1:27). Sin had not entered the garden, but the serpent beguiled the woman to taste of the fruit by distorting the scripture. Satan knew if they ate of the tree "in the midst of the garden" he could attempt to foil God's plan for mankind.

Satan's craftiness and purpose was to sabotage God's plan for mankind to live in a perfect union with God, living in sinless surroundings. Humanity became dogged by the curse of sin, yet God in His sovereignty destined mankind to be created in the image of God and for their ultimate redemption.

God's rightful position is his Lordship over our life. Satan will tempt us just as he did Eve, deceiving us to become as gods in control of our destiny and to know good and evil (Gen.3:5). This would give us licence to rule our lives with selfish ambition by putting the "I" on the throne of our lives above the place where God should be. This leads to pride, becoming gods in charge of our destiny and driven headlong to our downfall (Prov.16:18).

We become our own god when we wilfully choose to oppose God by sinning and harming our walk with Him. Our souls become unstable by this complacent attitude concerning the word of God. The Bible talks about "a double-minded man unstable in all his ways" (Jas.1:8).

The Double-minded Man

I recall how decades ago I lived an unstable and double-minded Christian life. I made excuses for my double-minded ways, eventually running out of excuses! I suffered acute satanic oppression, which drove me in conjunction with my wilful behaviour to turn from following Jesus. I was fearful of Satan's attacks and his fiery darts. I developed a depressive illness after a breakdown and burnout. This affected me spiritually, emotionally, and mentally.

Eve had a choice in the Garden of Eden to obey God's instructions, or not, and likewise we must make that choice, difficult as this may be.

The Bible shows how Eve was tempted. When she looked at the tree, it was inviting and she fell for the serpent's lies. The tree was "a tree desirable to make one wise" (Gen.3:6). Satan beguiled her to believe a lie that she could know wisdom if she ate of the fruit. She was aware of God's instructions in the Garden of Eden and what was required of her; but she was double-minded and unstable when she succumbed and ate of the forbidden fruit.

Pride – The Reason Satan Lost His Place in Heaven

We read about the downfall of Satan in Isaiah chapter 14. His pride cost his place in heaven. He was cast out of heaven by God when pride initiated an envious desire to be equal with Him. He wanted to *be* like Him and was not satisfied with his position in heaven.

"How you are fallen from heaven, O Lucifer, son of the morning! For you have said in your heart: I will ascend into heaven, I will exalt my throne above the stars of God; I will sit also on the mount of the congregation on the farthest sides of the north; I will ascend above the heights of the clouds; I will be like the Most High. Yet you shall be brought down to Sheol, to the lowest depths of the Pit." (Is.14:12-15). Satan's pride is clear in this passage of scripture with the repetitious use of "I".

Temptation and the False Covering

After Eve ate the forbidden fruit, she then gave it for her husband to eat. She was deceived by the serpent through the eye gate. First, she *saw* the fruit with her eyes, then she *desired* it and proceeded to fall into *temptation*.

Satan entices us by presenting sin as an alluring alterative to the claims and commands of God, even before we make the decision to deliberately sin. Trifling with the devil will always lead us into his trap. Sometimes we are lured by him because of a lack of knowledge and naïvety regarding his wiles and schemes. The word of God – when we study it, meditate on it, and memorise it – becomes our spiritual defence and weaponry against Satan. There is no shortcut or substitute.

What happens when we fall into Satan's trap and are tempted as Eve in the garden of Eden? Satan beguiles us and so we adopt a false covering to hide from God, just as Adam and Eve did in the garden. When Adam and Eve ate of the fruit, they knew they were naked and hid their nakedness by sewing fig leaves into aprons to cover themselves.

The fig leaves covering their nakedness could not hide the truth of their rebellion before God and spiritual nakedness in disobeying Him.

Sin Changes the Spiritual Dimension

After Adam and Eve made their choice to sin against God's command, the spiritual dimension immediately changed. Sin will always change the dimension in the spiritual realm. Adam and Eve were aware of their physical nakedness, but now they were spiritually naked too. The blessing of God had left them. Their sin had brought about the first judgement of God (Gen.3:14-19).

What is a false covering, then?

It can be tradition, a form of godliness, defined and shaped through piety. "...having a form of godliness but denying its power..." (2.Tim.3:5). A false form of godliness will always initiate a prideful attitude, through the upholding and preserving of a false spiritual reputation. It is a poor substitute for godly living and holiness. It is a counterfeit of true holiness. When we are clothed in the righteousness of God, we are aware of not being dependent upon self-effort.

The false covering may be defined as a false righteousness and occurs when we lean towards the flesh nature. This happens when we struggle for holiness of character in our own strength because we are misunderstanding the truth that "all of our righteous deeds are like a polluted garment." (Is.64:6).

The Fig of Self-Made Righteousness

Our 'fig leaf' coverings of self-made righteousness are filthy rags to God. They may appear to us as righteous coverings, but they are ineffectual and spiritually powerless to create holiness within us. They are manmade coverings after the fallen nature.

False coverings come in many disguises and pretences, and we are often deceived. We have all experienced this at some point in our Christian life because we are human. Like Adam and Eve, we adopt a false covering when we fail to see we are spiritually naked and blind, and, like Adam, we hide from the presence of God when He calls us.

Through wilful sin we become puffed up, seeing ourselves as 'gods'; in our selfish world we become prideful. We may not always recognise this trait, but if we do, God will not leave us in this blind spiritual state. He will allow us to see ourselves as spiritually wretched and naked before Him, because He is desirous to hone us into pure vessels in His image.

Knowing we are spiritually naked, hiding from God in areas of our life and adopting a false spiritual covering, will surely prevent us from behaving with integrity and transparency before God. It is impossible to walk truthfully in the power of the Holy Spirit whilst endeavouring to fix a spiritual situation or problem by carnal reasoning or conduct.

We are instructed to be "transformed by the renewing of our mind" (Rom.12:2). This renewal of our mind in alignment with Bible truth is where the answer to our circumstance should be sought and may be found.

Powerless Religion

"Then the eyes of both of them were opened, and they knew that they were naked: and they sewed fig leaves together and made themselves coverings." (Gen.3:7). Adam and Eve were mindful they had sinned against God, the lawgiver, and covered themselves in shame.

Conlon, in his article 'It's Time Again to Pray', clarifies this point by saying that people try "to cover their sin and shame in their own strength" when "darkness comes upon a society". I would suggest, they cover their sin and shame with their own type of fig leaf. They cannot hide from God and this is where God finds them in their shame.

The Fig Tree Rebellion

We read in Mark 11:13-14 Jesus speaks of Jerusalem having a 'fig tree religion', a religion of powerlessness which bears no fruit. The leaves on the fig tree were bountiful and so the tree should have flourished with an abundance of fruit, which it did not produce. Jesus uses this analogy to make a statement on the generation in His day, which had a religion requiring self-effort. As Jesus looked for fruit amongst the Jewish people he found none, and so He cursed the fig tree. Jesus said, "Let no one eat fruit from you ever again." (Mk.11:14). Peter's response on seeing the withered fig tree was, "Rabbi, look! The fig tree you cursed has withered away." (Mk.11:21).

The Apron as a False Covering

We read in Genesis 3:9 that God calls out to Adam, "Where are you?" God knew where Adam was! God is Omnipresent, but He longed to hear Adam's voice in response to His calling him. Adam panicked for he knew his sin could not be hidden from God. The fig leaf apron was a false covering which could never cover his sin. The false covering did not work for Adam and Eve and the false covering will not work for us either.

Adam may have tried to remedy the situation, but he was only too aware that he and his wife had transgressed. The aprons made from fig leaves were a feeble attempt to remedy a spiritual failing by carnal means. Our false coverings are inadequate, too, in restoring a rightful relationship and our spiritual standing in Christ.

We can adopt a false covering of religion which requires God's removal. This can only happen when we come under the searchlight of the Holy Spirit. God shedding a light on our hearts' motives lets us live as authentic witnesses for Christ, as God's children. We are fooled into thinking our fellowship with God is honest and our spiritual foundation secure on a sure footing, yet we often deceive ourselves. Passively we follow tradition and rituals which are familiar to us, and yet our hearts are far from God.

Instead of obeying God, like Adam and Eve we become spiritually blinded by the deception the serpent weaves. Adam and Eve were not truthful with God and consequently unable to discern spiritual truth about their situation and themselves. We are susceptible to fall into the same trap.

Our false coverings must be dealt with by God, in allowing the truth of who we were created to be in Christ to develop within us, and in forming a character of substance. This can only be experienced through a divine revelation in our spirit and by the Holy Spirit's empowering. We cannot progress spiritually unless we are clothed in and relying upon the righteousness of Christ, which is the only covering for the sin nature. No other covering will suffice.

Adam hid from the presence of God, afraid of what God's response to his sinning would be. He was aware of his physical nakedness, but even more keenly aware of his spiritual nakedness. God asked Adam who had told him he was naked and if he had eaten of the tree. His answer was ironical; he blamed the woman! God spoke to the woman who in turn blamed the serpent. She said, "The serpent deceived me, and I ate." (Gen.3:13).

When we hide behind a false covering, it is easy to attach blame to someone or something else. Taking responsibility for a false covering is the first step towards freedom and the removal of deception in an area of our life.

The scales fell from Eve's eyes after she had eaten the fruit and she observed the serpent as the beguiler he truly is. The devil's smooth, deceptive words propelled Eve to act contrary to God's commands for her life. We must be on our guard this does not happen to us.

We are human like Eve, and we may easily be deceived and tempted away from the truth God has spoken to us in the Bible. We must guard ourselves from adopting a false covering and when our hearts deceive us, remember the word of God, for here lies the truth to our questions and our circumstances. We are made in the image of God and His covering of righteousness, when appropriated in our lives, through Jesus' blood shed on the Cross, is enough and our true spiritual covering.

The devil is conniving in his mastery of a nation, seeking to trick and cause destruction. Our spiritual weapons against his tactics are in prayer. We are encouraged in 2 Corinthians 10:5 to "[cast] down imaginations, and every high thing that exalts itself against the knowledge of God, bringing every thought into captivity to the obedience of Christ". The spiritual weapons of a generation are employed through prayer and ensuring our thoughts on events and situations, as individuals and as a generation, align with scripture. We have the mind of Christ, and this should be a daily reality. Imaginings and thoughts which become exaggerated and wild in their intent, to entice us away from the truth of scripture, are deceptive and we are told to cast them down and bring them into captivity, in the name of Jesus. They are strongholds used by Satan to deceive us and as a generation.

Here we find our spiritual power in prayer. May God reveal to us our false coverings, so we may live transparent lives glorifying God by knowing our identity is in Christ.

Chapter Three

The Firm Foundation

WHEN CHRISTIANS FAMILIARISE THEMSELVES WITH SCRIPture, their obedience grows in allowing the Spirit of God to renew the mind. This is vital if our Christian walk is to be rooted on the firm foundation, which is Jesus Christ.

In Matthew 7:24-27 we read of the wise and foolish builders. We should take heed of the words Jesus spoke in the Gospel of Matthew for our spiritual roots to be embedded in good soil.

> *Therefore, whoever heareth these sayings of mine, and does them, I will liken him to a wise man which on that house; and it did not fall, for it was founded on the rock. but everyone who hears these built his house on the rock: and the rain descended, and the floods came, and the winds blew, and beat sayings of mine, and does not do them, will be like a foolish man who built his house on the sand: and the rain descended, and the floods came, and the winds blew, and beat on that house; and it fell. And great was its fall.*
>
> Matthew 7:24-27 (KJV)

Michael Green states, "After all we all need to know we belong. No man can erect a building of any serious dimensions on a rickety foundation. It would not be possible to live a Christian life on the shifting sand of doubt as to our relationship with our lord."[10]

He adds further, "...it is not modest to say, 'I hope I am a Christian, but I cannot say more.'" 1 Corinthians 1:30 assures us that we are saved by grace. Green asserts, "It is not, therefore, presumptuous to say with quiet confidence, 'I know that I belong to Christ. I have not done anything to earn it, but God has given me the Spirit and accepted me into

---

[10] Michael Green; *I Believe in the Holy Spirit;* p.80.

his family; and he means me to know that I belong.' The Spirit assures us – through signs."

Christians may ask themselves whether their faith is built on the Rock, Christ Jesus, or whether they are unstable and tossed with every tempest which seeks to overwhelm. Let us be realistic; this can easily happen and none of us are exempt from trials and temptations. It is how we react in the trial and view our circumstance which is of importance to God. Trials will assail, temptations beckon us, and like Eve we may be lured by the serpent's pleasant fruit he dangles in front of our eyes.

In the fiery trial when our faith is sorely tested, negative emotions often get the better of us. Fear, apprehension, anxiety and bewilderment are normal reactions to tragedies and adversity. It could be a death in the family, redundancy, or maybe financial woes we encounter. The problems and trials we face are vast.

Taking Up Our Cross

I share here my fiery trial of ill health. This was a trial of endurance and persistent pain. My body experienced physical pain on a level which I had never previously encountered. The pain immobilised me.

> I suffered rheumatic and arthritic pain in my joints. I was incapable of walking upstairs unaided. I climbed the stairs by hauling my body upwards sitting on the stairs and by climbing stair by stair. The debilitating symptoms progressed as the months passed. I had lapses in my memory which were frightening. My hair thinned, which all my life had had a thick texture. I had never been overweight, but now I put on two and a half stone. My frame which was naturally slim became huge. This puzzled me as I was not overeating. I presumed the symptoms indicated I had a chronic illness, but the doctor could not find a cause.
>
> My appointment with a neurologist and arthritic specialists did not resolve my health problems. The tests proved negative; nevertheless, my body continued to exhibit signs of multiple sclerosis and arthritis. The doctors and specialists I visited were ambiguous on a diagnosis and why my body showed indicators of various illnesses.
>
> One month became two and two became six, and soon a year had passed. Friends and family were accustomed to my walking with a stick. I spent well over a year unable to venture further than the garden gate.

My solace through my ill health was that if the medical profession did not have an answer to what was wrong with me physically then God certainly did. I was prescribed a large quantity of medication by my doctor. The irritable bowel condition triggered repeated retching at night. On many occasions I was admitted by ambulance to hospital. The medical staff did not discover a solution to aid my recovery from these debilitating ailments. After admittance to the hospital I was sent home, yet I was still no further forward in obtaining an answer to what was wrong with me.

When Christian friends saw I was not improving, they prayed with me in my house. My right leg was now very feeble and over the months it was bent inwards in a crooked position from the knee joint. I was unable to place my foot flat on the ground to walk unless God would heal me.

After friends prayed for my leg it miraculously straightened out. With encouragement I walked precariously but with baby steps. This healing process in my leg was amazing, not least because my legs had developed a weakness where I was unable to stand for long periods.

My stick remained my loyal friend I relied on to walk indoors, and from that day of prayer I no longer walked as a cripple. My leg from my knee downwards straightened.

This was the first tangible sign God was performing a healing work in my body. If I was not healed from all illness in the timescale I envisaged, I knew I should trust God's promises in the Bible for my healing.

I questioned my faith and asked myself whether my faith was built upon the Rock, Christ Jesus. My faith and trust in God were fundamental to my healing. I knew the choice remained as to whether I should submit to God and trust Him to heal me or allow negative emotions to rule my thoughts and decide the outcome.

God drew my attention to the verses in Matthew 7:24-27. It would have been so easy for me to give in to a root of bitterness and anger against God as to why He had allowed this feebleness in my body, but that would not have helped my spiritual outlook. I spent days where the pain was exhausting and many a sleepless night.

Ultimately, I knew God's plan was restoration of my health and not for me to deteriorate to the extent it would necessitate my use of a wheelchair. I trusted God's sovereignty over my life.

The results from a routine blood test revealed my thyroxine level in my body was extremely low. The blood test confirmed I was suffering from a very underactive thyroid. This condition should have been diagnosed and treated years previously with a hospital blood test and prescription medication from a doctor.

God was testing my faith in the trial, and trust in God developed through my debility. He had taught me much.

I read my Bible during this fiery trial, whilst sapped of physical energy. I dwelt on passages of scripture which instilled hope and encouragement in me, and I felt God strengthening my faith. I was growing through God's purifying fire.

Take Up Your Cross

The Bible instructs the Christian, "Whoever desires to come after Me, let him deny himself, and take up his cross and follow Me." (Mk.8:34).

Watchman Nee writes about denying our self and the truth about evading it.[11] The Bible says that such a person "is not worthy of [Jesus]" if he doesn't deny himself (Matt.10:38), for "he cannot be My disciple" (Lk.14:27).

We must not avoid the crosses we have to bear, but rather embrace them as tools in God's hands for change. Our cross can be a training ground if we commit the cross and trial to God. Our spiritual growth is God's aim. Christians should continually experience the act of putting to death the deeds of the flesh and our earthy desires and needs, instead living by faith through the resurrection power of the Cross. Keeping the power of the Cross as our focus when we reach a crossroads in our life, when devoid of strength, enables us to become transformed by replacing our weakness with His strength. We will never be the same again when our service for God is revolutionised. Our service for God will no longer be dependent on our strength, but trusting in God's strength, we overcome and serve others.

God deals with Jacob, which we read of in the biblical account. Jacob has cheated his brother Esau out of his birthright, and to escape the murderous wrath of Esau he escapes to Haran to live with a relative, Laban. It is here Jacob finds a wife. Jacob tries to amend his estrangement from Esau and sends on ahead three convoys of presents. The family cross

---

[11] Watchman Nee; *The Normal Christian Life*.

the dangerous river of Jabbok leaving Jacob who decides to earnestly pray alone to God.

It is here Jacob grapples with a man in the form of an angel. Jacob has strived against God's will for him all his life. He has wrestled Esau over the birthright, and now he finds himself faced with a man in the form of an angel wrestling him all night.

God wrestles Jacob for his compliance. God is desirous for something from Jacob, which was is submission to Him, but this can only happen when God has Jacob's attention and he is unaccompanied, wrestling Him.

Jacob, in fear of Esau and his murderous intent, has been desperate to sort out his problems his way, and the only way God can gain Jacob's attention is in causing Jacob's hip to dislocate with an injury, causing him hereafter to walk with a limp.

Now Jacob's focus turns to God, knowing he has been face to face with Him, and recognising his helplessness, with no strength to wrestle God anymore. It is here Jacob comes to the end of himself, and with his strength gone he implores of God for a blessing in his weakness. God forces Jacob to submit to Him, and says his name, which He changes to Israel.

Jacob learnt his strength came from God, and not from himself. He always walked with a limp after this encounter and it was a reminder of his wrestle with God. He learnt that his strength could only be realised in submitting to God's will, and in his weakness came to know his strength was found in God alone.

Jacob named the place where he wrestled with God 'Penuel' which means the 'face of God'.

The account of Jacob reminds us that we too should submit wholly to God's lordship over our life. God often takes us down obscure roads and we may find after our struggle with God that we too, like Jacob, will walk with our own 'limp' – but it will forever be a reminder to us, when we let go of the reins of our life and submit wholly to the lordship of God, that in our weakness we truly find God is our strength.

In many ways I could relate to Jacob as I journeyed through my illness. Knowing my feebleness, I did not possess the will to fight my disease or achieve what I was certain God wanted for my life. I, like Jacob, found myself in a frustrating place, until I spiritually awoke and recognised I needed to die to my plans in the situation. It was the beginning of God's strengthening and I could cope with my inability to

The Firm Foundation

walk when I understood the bigger picture of God's hand and guidance sovereign over my life. The question remained, were my spiritual roots planted on the firm foundation, which is Christ, or was I sinking in the sand?

How do we grasp hold of God's strength in our weakness? The answer lies in the truth that death always precedes the resurrection, as with the Cross of Jesus.

A Christian must deny himself and take up his cross if he is going to be a disciple of Jesus. Watchman Nee explains that God will take us through "difficult and painful ways in order to get us there".

> *If you endure chastening, God deals with you as with sons; for what son is there whom a father does not chasten?*
>
> Hebrews 12:7

> *Therefore whoever hears these sayings of Mine, and does them, I will liken him to a wise man who built his house upon a rock: and the winds blew and beat on that house; and it did not fall, for it was founded on the rock.*
>
> Matthew 7:24,25

I did not want to fail in trusting God in my ill health, or grumble in the wilderness experience of pain and suffering. Like Eve, I could have blamed the serpent or someone else for my demise, or like Adam who blamed his wife for tempting him to eat of the forbidden fruit.

Attaching blame to someone or something would have meant wrapping myself in an apron of deceit, a false covering, and fooling myself by reacting carnally in adversity. I knew God wanted a loftier way for me which was found in my identification with Christ's sufferings on the Cross.

Watchman Nee explains the experience as God founding a new status within us of "resurrection ground"[12]. It is a place where what you have lost has been affected but now you understand it in a different way, with "new values become under heaven's control".

This new status of "resurrection ground" is true for all Christians who face fiery trials and temptation. Trials will inevitably be present in seasons of our lives. It is helpful to re-evaluate our spiritual walk. Are we

---

[12] Watchman Nee; *The Normal Christian Life;* p.177.

wise, "rightly dividing the word of truth", or are we like the unwise builder in Matthew 7:24-27?

We may permit negative emotions to surface which will crush the life of God within us, or the cares of this world and worldly pursuits which choke the seed. We will then be poorly equipped to overcome in God's power to face our trials with fortitude.

What is the way through the fiery trial? It is natural to grieve when going through a bereavement, or in the humiliation of monetary loss, for example. We face a myriad of problems and we often fail in our perception as to what our position as victors in Christ is, bought for us on the Cross.

Our dilemmas loom with threatening menace to overcome us. We can relate to Job who had his unsympathetic comforters for friends, when we must navigate a pessimistic response from our friends. It is true that God can change our circumstances, but often He changes *us* in the fiery trial.

The Sower and the Seed

I believe the answer lies at the start of our Christian walk with the Lord. What does the Bible teach about spiritual roots needing to be planted deeply within the soil of our faith? In Matthew 13:3-9 Jesus spoke in a parable to the crowds about a sower sowing his seed.

Jesus often spoke in parables to those who gathered to hear Him speak. In this parable Jesus used the soil as an illustration to get across His message. A sower plants his seeds, and grows crops; therefore, it made perfect sense Jesus would use an earthy substance such as the soil and the seed, so familiar in the daily lives of people in biblical times, to reach out to the hearts of men. By making this connection between the sower and the seed, Jesus could expound on spiritual truth.

Some seeds fell by the wayside and were eaten by the fowls. Some fell on places that were stony with little earth. They sprung up because the earth was shallow. The sun scorched the plants and they withered because they had no roots. Some of the seed fell onto ground that was good, which yielded fruit, some a hundredfold, some sixtyfold, some thirtyfold.

In Matthew 13:19-23 Jesus explains to his disciples the spiritual meaning behind His parable of the sower and the seed.

The seed which fell by the wayside are those who heard the word of God but did not understand its meaning. The devil came along and snatched away the word that was sown in their heart.

Others received the seed into stony places and received it joyfully. However, because there was no root in this one, when persecution or trials came because of the word, they became offended.

Still others received the seed amongst the thorns. They heard the word, but the cares of the world and riches choked the word and they were not fruitful.

Those who received the word into good soil, heard it and comprehended it, brought forth fruit, some hundredfold, some sixty and some thirty.

In Matthew 13:19 we read that when the seed is not understood by the hearer, and the roots do not go deeply into the soil, the devil snatches the word away from them. How important it is when Christians share their faith to ensure the hearer of the gospel grasps the meaning of the gospel (Jn.3:16).

We read that this seed is sown into someone's life, but the devil wasted no time in robbing the gospel seed which he showed interest in. "This is he who received seed by the wayside." (Matt.13:19). This soul does not reach the place where he can be discipled in the Christian faith.

The second illustration of the sower and the seed is the one who receives the gospel seed in stony places. However, the root does not go down deep into the soil, even though at first the seed is received with joy.

Unfortunately, when trouble or persecution comes to this soul, he becomes offended with the gospel. This soul must be taught the Christian walk is not one of ease, that when you come to Jesus your problems will not automatically be solved! It is advisable that mature Christians of faith disciple the new Christian soon after conversion.

Repentance – Turning Away from the Old Ways

I tell you, no; but unless you repent, you will all likewise perish.

Luke 13:3

Therefore, if anyone is in Christ, he is a new creation; old things have passed away; behold, all things have become new.

2 Corinthians 5:17

We make a choice to turn from the old way of life and live a spiritual life with Christ at the centre. This means embracing the new life through the Holy Spirit's empowering. The new Christian has been quickened within through the spiritual birth. This spiritual path has allowed the truth of the gospel message to be discerned by the power of the Holy Spirit. The new believer must learn to stand on the firm foundation, which is the Rock, Christ Jesus.

During these initial stages of a relationship with Jesus, it would be helpful if the new Christian would be nurtured by a mature Christian, who can explain the scriptures and what has occurred at conversion in the new believer's spirit. The new believer must understand what their decision and commitment to follower Jesus will mean in their life and the changes which will follow in their lifestyle.

A new believer, when guided through the discipling process, will usually have an enquiring mind on spiritual things and a desire to read the Bible. They will start to benefit from discussions on biblical doctrine and commands in the Bible, so they may grow in faith. They will be taught what is their spiritual position in Christ. Possessing a basic grounding in the Christian faith will strengthen the new believer from turning back in his walk with God, especially when he faces difficulties.

Michael Green speaks of the change which should happen when someone has the Holy Spirit indwelling within them. He says this believer "keeps God's word" or "walks as Christ walked" (1.Jn.2:5,6).

Green accepts of the fact that it takes time for someone to change and that they do not "become sinless overnight". However, he emphasises that after they are adopted as Christ's heirs in the kingdom of God, according to Romans 8, there is a change in their actions, "radiated by the Spirit" of God, which is manifested "in a change of behaviour".

A Way Out of Temptation

> *No temptation has overtaken you except but such as is common to man; but God is faithful, who will not allow you to be tempted beyond what you are able, but with the temptation will also make the way of escape, that you may be able to bear it.*
>
> 1 Corinthians 10:13

This verse clearly shows we will all be tempted at times. It is "common to man", and being tempted is not a sin. Jesus was tempted in the wilderness, yet without sin (Matt.4:1-11).

Sometimes our difficulties may not resolve straightaway. For example, we may be persecuted for following Jesus. We know we feel the pressure when people oppose our Christian beliefs. It is then that those weaker in the faith are tempted to throw the towel in! They may be tempted to sin in an area of their life and are lured away from the Lord's commands.

Our spiritual foundation should be rooted in good soil, and we will not be offended or ashamed of the gospel. There is no turning back for the Christian from following Christ when things appear to go pear-shaped! We are forgiven by Jesus if we fall into sin and if we repent, and he will restore us to Himself. We do not need to live in condemnation.

We understand the importance for a new believer to read the scriptures which are for his growth and encouragement. God wants new believers standing on the promises of God, so they grow in faith and experience that they are overcomers through the power of God.

I wonder if the outcome of the weaker Christian who is tempted to flounder in his faith would be different if he were discipled by a mature believer to understand that the Christian journey involves dying to self and the way of the Cross.

Let us look at the seed in the parable of the sower more fully. The Bible, in the parable of the seed and the sower, explains that when trials came it caused those affected to be offended by the gospel message. The person who firstly received the seed with joy, later became disenchanted with the gospel through trials or persecution.

It may be argued that unless a Christian is nurtured in his faith to understand God's dealings with him in his trials, a danger remains of losing the joy firstly received with the planting of the seed! How crucial it is for a new Christian to be discipled well.

Victory is secure in the name of Jesus alone and through the power of the Cross. We may rest assured knowing, as Green explains, that the Spirit which lives within the believer "mediates to them the victory over the world" (1.Jn.4:4).

This is the same victory Jesus had which is available to us to today. We can overcome temptation and endure our trials by the power of the Cross and the Holy Spirit.

Persecuted for Christ

I share here of my experience on temptation as a new Christian.

I was surrounded by a dormitory of girls in boarding school who opposed my sharing the gospel. It was not unusual to be physically assaulted for my faith. On one occasion my Bible was thrown out of the window.

My interest in the gospel happened unexpectedly when a fellow pupil shared with me at school. Late one evening I knelt in front of a dormitory of pupils and confessed my need of a Saviour. In my mind's eye I saw Jesus pierced on the Cross of Calvary for all the wrong I had committed. I saw in my mind's eye the fighting, the spiritualism, cursing and my hardened heart. I repented of my sin and went to bed peacefully for the first time in my young life. I knew I was forgiven and washed in the blood of Jesus.

I was ready from the start of my Christian journey, if necessary, to face ridicule from my peers for my faith. I withstood the taunts and physical assaults railed against me. What helped was that the pupil who shared the gospel with me explained to me clearly that the Christian life was not going to be an easy road.

I boarded at a vocational school and it had crossed my mind that maybe God would require me to forsake my aspirations of becoming a dancer to follow Him. I would certainly have to hold my ground in not taking the pupils' offences personally. I had experienced the divine love of Jesus and I had never felt anything like this before.

I took the taunts, although reluctantly at times, and when tested for my faith I loved my peers in return, demonstrating this with my actions. I was not special, nor could I forgive easily, but I trusted Jesus to fill me with His Holy Spirit and so I was able to love in response to the ridicule. The love of Jesus empowered me, for my love was extremely poor in comparison to the unconditional love of Jesus.

As a believer we will all face the world's opposition to our faith in varying degrees. The Bible warns us not to be disconcerted by the world's reaction to our faith in God.

"Do not marvel my brethren, if the world hates you." We also know that we have passed from death to life because "we love the brethren" (1.Jn.3:13,14).

Sharing the Gospel

The gospel seed was sown in my heart when I heard the gospel message for the first time. This seed went deeply into the soil of my soul. My friend prepared me by sharing with me God's commands, His statutes and precepts. She taught me these even before I had committed my life to Jesus.

When we are born again of the Spirit of God, there should be a noticeable change of direction immediately after conversion in wanting to change our lifestyle and the negative influences around us. Of course, we do not become perfect overnight! The light of Jesus' saving grace nevertheless should be evident and seen in the new believer.

The new convert is eager to share their faith with unbelievers, just as the gospel has been shared with them. We do not have to wait until we know all the answers before we share our faith.

The novice believer is acutely aware of having received the witness of the Spirit with their own spirit that they are God's child (Rom.8:16). There is knowledge of a change having occurred within themselves, which is the quickening of the Holy Spirit within them through the 'born again' experience.

Jesus has given them a new heart; they are a new creation, and their heart longs to follow Jesus and be like Him. This new Christian is desirous for the seed they share to be good seed. Their purpose is that the seed will be planted deeply within the soil of the hearer.

The Spirit Himself witnesses with our spirit that we are God's children, and we can be assured we belong to Christ.[13] Michael Green notes, "In 1 Thessalonians 1:5 Paul reminds his readers how the gospel was first preached to them: 'it came not in word only, but in power and in the Holy spirit and in full assurance'." He continues, "...the literal meaning seems to be that a man is so full of the Holy Spirit that he carries conviction when he speaks about Christ. Christian assurance is not merely intellectual persuasion but an overwhelming convincing experience of the indwelling Spirit welling up within us and flowing out to others. Such is the confidence that the Spirit means to give believers."[14]

Christians should actively seek to be fruitful for the kingdom of God. We have searched and found in the parable of the sower and the seed

---

[13] *Ibid.*
[14] Michael Green; *I Believe in the Holy Spirit;* p.82.

that the problem lies in the seed being snatched away with the hearing of the gospel message. The cares of this world and trials stop the fruition of the seed's existence from being embedded in the soil of the hearer's heart.

The devil is keen to snatch the word of God away from the hearer by undermining the gospel message in rendering it unproductive in the hearts and minds of those who would receive salvation. We should not be put off from speaking about Jesus because of this. God can save to the uttermost.

In my Christian experience, I understood the significance of identifying with the Cross soon after my conversion. The pupil who led me to Jesus did not dress up salvation as a quick fix to solve the problems in my life, or a way to a trouble-free life! In fact, she told me the exact opposite: that it would require boldness to speak of the good news which had transformed my life, and to share my faith immediately!

When the seed is received by the hearer in good soil, it will go on to produce fruit for the kingdom of God. This is the outworking of the Holy Spirit within the believer who has been grafted into the vine.[15]

---

[15] See John 15

Chapter Four

Growing in Christ and the Cost of Discipleship

1. Adopted into God's Family (A New Creation in Christ)

After we receive God's gift of salvation, God adopts us into His family. What a wonderful experience this is. We are no longer orphans!

The pupil who instructed me to salvation was my sister in Christ. This was a new concept to me. I was shown the following scripture verse from the Bible:

> *For you did not receive the spirit of bondage again to fear, but you received the Spirit of adoption by whom we cry out, Abba, Father.*
>
> *Romans 8:15*

We are God's children, adopted by Him, and as His children our response is, "Abba, Father." God is my heavenly Father; and He is yours if you have been born again into the kingdom of God (Jn.3; Rom.6:23).

My friend explained I was a new creation in Christ Jesus from the moment I accepted Jesus' forgiveness for my sin and asked Him into my life.

> *Therefore, if anyone is in Christ, he is a new creation; old things have passed away; behold all things have become new.*
>
> *2 Corinthians 5:17*

I was a forgiven child of God. I had been brought into the kingdom of God by the precious blood of Jesus. I was now born again of the Spirit of God and adopted into His kingdom. There are billons of brothers and sisters in Christ who, like me, have been adopted into the family of God! The wonder of it all!

2. Knowing Our Position in Christ

The second spiritual truth I learnt from my friend who discipled me, was to grasp what had occurred to me with the new birth mentioned in John chapter 3. I was educated to learn what my spiritual position meant in my spiritual walk with Jesus.

My identity was in Christ and I was to abide in the vine, spoken of in John chapter 15. I learnt that God viewed me not as a sinner now but as a Christian and forgiven through the blood of Jesus shed at Calvary (Rom.6:2).

My spiritual standing in Christ was based on the truth in the Bible. I had no wish to follow the patterns of this world. I knew within my spirit I was raised up with Christ to know His glory and holiness.

> *...even when we were dead in trespasses, made us alive together with Christ (by grace you have been saved), and raised us up together, and made us sit together in the heavenly places in Christ Jesus.*
>
> *Ephesians 2:5,6*

When we are moved to seek after God, this is in response to His wooing us to Himself first. This stirring in our heart to know God originates from a revelation and knowledge in our spirit that when Jesus was nailed to the Cross as a sacrifice for our sin, that sin was dealt with once and for all. The conversion experience is an act of surrender to Christ and it is where a quickening in our spirit takes place, in knowing our sin was nailed to the Cross with Christ. We are sure we have been resurrected with Him in newness of life, to sit in heavenly places with Christ.

Furthermore, I learnt that my spiritual standing in Christ meant the devil was under my feet. I no longer need to allow sin to dominate my actions by accommodating the carnal nature, or dwelling in fear as I had previously, because Jesus had triumphed over all the power of the enemy when He rose again and defeated death.

> *But thanks be to God, who gives us the victory through our Lord Jesus Christ.*
>
> *1 Corinthians 15:57*

I walked in the truth of God's word that I was an overcomer through the power of the Cross and no more was I to rely on my own strength;

Growing in Christ and the Cost of Discipleship

because Jesus had overcome, so I had overcome by the power of His blood.

For those who persevere and overcome in this life, they will know eternally that "he who overcomes shall inherit all things, and I will be his God, and he shall be my son" (Rev.21:7).

> *To him who overcomes I will I grant to sit with Me on My throne, as I also overcame and am sat down with my Father on His throne.*
>
> Revelation 3:21

My friend taught me I possessed the same authority over Satan as Jesus. When I was tempted, if I put God first in my life by submitting to His authority and resisting Satan, the devil would depart from me.

> *Therefore submit to God. Resist the devil and he will flee from you.*
>
> James 4:7

By faith we are to dress in the whole armour of God (Eph.6:11-18). It is essential we are equipped and ready to fight the enemy, staying alert through the Holy Spirit's power, whilst mindful of the origin of spiritual attack. We ought to develop a keen spiritual interest in discerning the fiery darts of the enemy when they attack us and be knowledgeable of the devil's schemes.

We are to remain observant by looking for opportunities to share our faith, prepared with our feet shod with the gospel of peace. For the committed Christian who walks keenly with God, there is a vigilance to discern Satan's schemes and wiles. When a believer is mindful of sin's unattractiveness and its pull to lead him into bondage, he will decide to embrace the armour of God for his protection.

3. The Baptism in the Holy Spirit

My experience when I repented of my sin, kneeling on the dormitory floor at boarding school, was, I knew with a certainty, that Jesus had washed away my sin through His shed blood and forgiven me, and I would inherit eternal life (Rom.6:23).

Five days after my conversion experience, I was baptised in the Holy Spirit. My friend who had committed her life to Christ and experienced the fullness of the Holy Spirit all on the same day of her conversion, was eager I should waste no time in receiving the baptism in the Holy Spirit too!

It would be fitting at this point to explore the Holy Spirit's power and infilling.

> *But you shall receive power when the Holy Spirit has come upon you; and you shall be witnesses to me in Jerusalem, and in all Judea and Samaria and to the end of the earth.*
>
> Acts 1:8

Acts 1:5 says, "Ye shall be baptised with the Holy Ghost not many days hence." The baptism in the Holy Spirit is a separate experience available for all believers to receive after salvation. In Acts 1:5 we read they were instructed " to wait for the promise of the Father". In Acts 2:4 we read, "And they were all filled with the Holy Spirit and began to speak in tongues as the Spirit gave them utterance." Therefore Acts 2:4 was the fulfilment of the promise in Acts 1:5 of the fullness of the Holy Spirit which they would receive. It was another experience. Another scripture confirming the fullness of the Holy Spirit, also called the baptism in the Holy Spirit in Acts 2:4, is Acts 11:15,16. In verse 15 we read that the Holy Spirit "fell on them" and verse 16 says, "John indeed baptised with water, but you shall be baptised with the Holy Spirit."

I will briefly recall my experience when I received the baptism in the Holy Spirit.

> I knew a boldness after my baptism in the Holy Spirit experience, which I did not possess in me naturally, to share with others of my faith and the saving power of Jesus. I introduced my friends to the gospel account of Nicodemus in John chapter 3, who was a religious ruler of his day.
>
> I was not intimidated by my peers as I spoke with them and it was never a struggle for me to find the correct words or terminology conversing on matters of faith. The relevant scripture verses popped into my mind when I needed them in answer to many a probing question.
>
> I knew without any doubt that the baptism in the Holy Spirit quickened me with a boldness to witness as the Christians in the book of Acts knew. It was soon after this all-encompassing experience that I led my school friends to Christ and very soon I prayed for them to be baptised in the Holy Spirit and they received the baptism too.

Growing in Christ and the Cost of Discipleship

> My eyes were drawn to the scripture in 1 Corinthians 12:4-11 on the gifts of the Holy Spirit. This became noticeably clear to me. The joyful, exuberance from the Lord, which my friend radiated, was rubbing off on me!
>
> Here I was, only five months since first hearing the gospel, and with my recent conversion I was earnestly desiring the gifts of the Holy Spirit for myself. I was thirsty for all God's blessings He wanted to lavish upon me, and I was sure if I asked Jesus in faith for the gifts of the Holy Spirit, He would answer my prayer.
>
> Two months after my conversion I spoke in tongues out loud and fluently. Soon after this experience I received the gift of prophecy. I was fifteen years old. It was not long after this that my sister and I were actively using the gifts of tongues, prophecy and interpretation of tongues in our local Pentecostal Church in our hometown, during the school holidays! Nothing could hold us back!

My hopes are that in recalling my encounter of the Holy Spirit's infilling and the scriptures on the baptism in the Holy Spirit, that you too will know the validity of this experience.

The baptism in the Holy Spirit empowers the Christian with strength in the inward man to withstand temptation. It opens the spiritual eyes to know Jesus personally in a fuller way, up until now not previously encountered. A closer relationship with Jesus develops with the fullness of the Holy Spirit.

It is no longer a case of seeking by self-effort to impute righteousness. The Holy Spirit fills to overflowing when we earnestly seek Him in prayer to "stir up the gift" within us (2.Tim.1:6). A new dimension opens, walking in the Holy Spirit, in which we do not strive to please God legalistically through our own righteousness.

Wisdom is needed when we disciple a new Christian in introducing them to the scriptures regarding the baptism in the Holy Spirit. We should not wait weeks, months, or even years before receiving. A new believer, open to the fullness of the Holy Spirit and walking uprightly with God, may receive soon after conversion. The novice Christian is less likely to fall away from the Christian path if he is rooted and grounded in the faith and aware of the glory and presence of Jesus at the beginning of their Christian road.

Pat Regan's Account of His Baptism in the Holy Spirit

Here is Pat Regan's account of his experience on how he received the baptism in the Holy Spirit. Pat is a mature believer of many years.

> I came from a background of abuse and religion. I became aware of the manifestations of the Holy Spirit whilst attending another church and hearing believers speaking in an unknown language, which up until that time was foreign to me. A believer in the congregation gave an interpretation and this had a profound effect on my Christian faith, that a Christian could have a close relationship with the God of heaven; furthermore, that God would speak in a direct and personal way in a service.
>
> I was already born of the Spirit. My experience was an amazing one and was not dissimilar to that of the disciples when Jesus breathed on them and they received eternal life (Jn.20:20).
>
> Acts 1:5 says, after the resurrection of Jesus, "...you shall be baptized with the Holy Spirit not many days hence." This was new to me. I hadn't realised up until this time that there was a second experience of the Holy Spirit. This experience was like being baptised in water, but fully immersed; a baptism of the Holy Spirit. This baptism was a baptism of power when the Holy Spirit comes upon a person (Acts.1:8).
>
> I was so hungry for more of God that I eagerly attended what was known then as a 'waiting' meeting, where we had hands laid on us to receive the baptism in the Holy Spirit.
>
> For over four years I attended countless 'waiting' meetings where all I felt happen was my head became shinier, so many people had laid hands on my head! I would not give up.
>
> It was while I was attending a Youth Camp in my teens and I was standing outside yet another 'waiting' meeting that the Lord spoke to my heart, "You will receive tonight." With that word I joined the others in the tent meeting, where I sat on a hard bench, and it was then that an overwhelming presence of God began to flood my whole body and soul. It was like I was drowning in liquid love and power. Almost immediately I began to speak in another language. There was so much joy and a sense of being cleansed, like I was in a shower, saturated with the person of the Holy Spirit. The union of God's heart and my own was like a fusion of being welded together.

Somehow the darkness went with this light and I could see with the eyes of my heart more clearly. I was conscious that there was a power within that would equip me to fulfil God's call on my life. I would no longer feel like an orphan.

This sensitivity to the love of God and the guidance I needed in life as I embarked on this journey of faith increased, like the fine tuning of a radio.

With hindsight and spiritual experience, I have come to realise the doctrine I had been taught earlier in my Christian walk was wrong. I did not have to wait to receive the baptism in the Holy Spirit, but only to ask and to receive it. This was my heavenly Father's gift to me, His child (Lk.24:49).

I have eternal life, but not only this but a river of Life that flows out of me to fulfil God's purpose in my life.

Pat Regan

4. Strengthened in the Inner Man

> *...that he would grant you according to the riches of his glory, to be strengthened with might through His Spirit in the inner man, that Christ may dwell in your hearts through faith; that you, being rooted and grounded in love, may be able to comprehend with all the saints what is the width, and length, and depth and height – to know the love of Christ, which passes knowledge; that you may be filled with all the fulness of God.*
>
> *Ephesians 3:16-19*

God wants the Christian strengthened in their inner man. "For you died, and your life is hid with Christ in God." (Col.3:3). We are dead to our old carnal nature and were spiritually quickened when we were born again of the Spirit. When Christ was crucified and died on the Cross, it was here our old carnal nature died on the Cross with Him. Christ took you and me to the Cross when He died, and we died with Him there.

At conversion we pass from spiritual death into spiritual life. We were destined to an eternity in hell, separated from Christ, and are now brought into an eternal life with God (Rom.6:23). God desires the Christian to recognise the truth of this, because our life is not our own to live as we please; it "is hidden with Christ in God" (Col.3:3).

When a person is born again, they become a new person. The indwelling Christ resides within them.

The Christian is encouraged to grow in Christ and be strengthened in their spirit, as we read in Ephesians. We are strengthened within our spirit knowing without doubting the love of God, and knowing "the width, and length, depth and height" of God's love (Eph.3:18).

We find, when a new believer is discipled by mature Christians into an encounter with Jesus, through prayer and Bible study, there is a notable change in their attitude towards God and others. A fervent thirst develops for spiritual things.

I found this to be true when mature believers encouraged me to seek Christ in praying out loud immediately after I became a born-again Christian and to read the Bible in my personal devotions. This helped me to know my focus was primarily on God whilst praying out loud, and I was not easily distracted when other people prayed around me.

My desire remained to press in spiritually beyond the veil and experience the glory of God. My friend led by example, though she was young in years. She discipled me and I went on to experience for myself the love of God more fully.

Ephesians 3:18 talks of the strength in the inner man of a Christian who is rooted and grounded in Christ. This revelation in our spirit reveals to us our security in Christ, and it is He who is the true and firm foundation.

As we stand on the word of God in faith, we are strengthened in our spirit. The promises of God are not a dead letter, but the written, inspired and infallible living word of God, which builds faith in the believer.

The promises of God exist to aid us in our trials by focusing our spiritual sights on God and not on ourselves. This act of discipline frees us to walk steadfastly through our trials with God at the helm. This is something which only the Holy Spirit can create. It is not dependent upon our fluctuating emotions. The promises of God are for our edification, encouragement, and strengthening in our inner man.

The book of James reveals that when we persevere through trials it enables a growth in faith and empowers us with inner strength. From the outset of his letter we read that there is "a testing of your faith" (Jas.1:2), a process of journeying though "various trials" which we meet. Furthermore, he speaks in this verse as though trials are not something to throw us off balance! Trials are indicative of God desiring a growth in faith and joy through it. We are encouraged to "count it all joy" (v.2).

Growing in Christ and the Cost of Discipleship

The lesson of counting it all joy goes against the carnal man's natural tendency. It is a necessary lesson we should learn, however, for patience is produced through the testing of our faith! James 1:3 endorses this, and in verse 4 we read that God is at work in the trial and we are "to let patience have its perfect work".

We can understand more clearly how this strengthening within creates the fruit of the Spirit within us to blossom, shaped by trials and temptations, so "that you be perfect and complete, lacking nothing".

By the finished work of the Cross we have received everything pertaining to life in the Holy Spirit.

We stand complete in Christ because God's word is enough to keep, strengthen, and uphold us in our trials. We are perfect in Christ, justified, and sanctified.

Our strengthening in the inner man in trials originates when we have a total trust and reliance on God, and the knowledge "that you may be perfect and complete, lacking nothing". This is true because "your life is hidden with Christ in God" (Col.3:3).

Jesus is enough, and we cannot add to this by working things out through our own initiative. Everything we need in our time of need is found in the Bible and that includes the wisdom of God which is freely available to us.

If any of you lack wisdom, let him ask of God, who gives to all liberally and without reproach, and it will be given to him.

James 1:5

James tells us that God clearly uses our trials to strengthen us and create patience: "...but let patience have its perfect work." (v.4). We also find that wisdom is available in our trials and temptations. God has not left us as orphans struggling, for His wisdom is not "sensual, earthly", as the world's wisdom is. God's wisdom is given to us "liberally and without reproach" (v.5).

All of God's resources are at our disposal, empowering the Christian to be strengthened in his spirit so he can withstand the storms of life. We only grow spiritually as we journey through the fiery trial in learning to "count it all joy".

We will of course require the wisdom of God in making sense of trials in accordance with God's word, yet we will only receive wisdom if we do not doubt that we will receive this from God when we ask Him (v.6). James 1:6-8 warns us that "he who doubts is like a wave of the sea driven and tossed by the wind". Such a man as this we are warned must not "suppose that he will receive anything from the Lord". This person is "doubled-minded" and "unstable in all his ways".

If we ask God to strengthen us in our inner man, then we must allow Him to perfect His work within us, though this may require His correction. We must learn that perseverance in the trial is essential to build us up spiritually, which will bear fruit in our character and result in a greater faith in God.

We grow in our faith as we believe God hears and answers our requests and prayers that align with His precious promises.

> *Now faith is the substance of things hoped for; the evidence of things not seen.*
>
> Hebrews 11:1

Faith grasps hold of a promise before it is manifest and evidenced in our life. There is a knowledge that comes from God when we trust and have faith that what God has said He can do, He *will* perform.

> *...by which have been given to us exceedingly great and precious promises, that through these you may be partakers of the divine nature, having escaped the corruption that is in the world through lust.*
>
> 2 Peter 1:4

In this verse we are to understand the benefit of the promises of God, which are to lead us into holiness and for our sanctification.

We are to rely upon the promises of God as the infallible truth and in so doing we will reflect the divine nature when the promises of God are outworked in our life.

Once we were slaves to worldly desires and its lusts, and lived under Satan's domain, but now we have been set free.

> *Therefore, if the Son makes you free, you shall be free indeed.*
>
> John 8:36

5. Dying to Self

Colossians 3:8-10 shows the importance of putting off the old man, the deeds of the carnal nature, and putting on the new man, which is renewed after the image of Christ.

When I was a young Christian, dying to selfish desires and carnal deeds was relatively easy, because I loved Jesus and desired to obey His commands. Christians are to make a daily choice whether to live their life letting the carnal nature have control, by fulfilling the deeds of the flesh, or walking according to the regenerated nature (Jn.3).

Summary

We have seen how Jesus is the true foundation and cornerstone of our faith (Eph.2:2) and "the true vine" (Jn.15:1).

We have talked about the false coverings which Christians may use to conceal their failings to their detriment. It is all too easy to be unaware of Satan's deception as Adam and Eve were deceived. When Adam and Eve's eyes were opened in the garden of Eden to Satan's deception, they knew their disobedience had created a spiritual nakedness. We too adopt false coverings, often unwittingly. The book of Genesis reveals how false coverings come in many disguises and the significance of planting our spiritual feet on the Rock, Christ Jesus, and not on the sinking sand.

We discussed how Satan snatches the good seed from the hearer, so they are not planted in good soil. We also discussed the importance of discipleship for the new Christian.

We looked at how the believer presents the gospel message to the unbeliever, which can be misinterpreted. We explored that when this ensues it affects the seed and our spiritual roots which demand to be planted deeply in good soil.

We examined the Scriptures relating to discipleship, most crucially for the new believer and the implications on their decision to follow Christ, as this will impact on their commitment to Christ. I was taught the scriptures and discipled by my friend many decades ago in this way.

God is keen for the believer to bring forth good fruit.

> *He who continually goes forth weeping, bearing seed for sowing, shall doubtless come again with rejoicing, bringing his sheaves with him.*
>
> *Psalm 126:6*

This verse in Psalm 126 is the wish of every dedicated Christian who has tasted and seen that the Lord is good. May it always be the prayer of our hearts and our desire as pure vessels to bear fruit for the kingdom of God.

Article on Discipleship

Here is Pastor Keith Brown's article on 'Discipleship'. Keith Brown is pastor of Southend Full Gospel Church, Southend, UK.

Of the many people who come to our Lord and get saved, only a few will go on to true discipleship, perhaps through ignorance, or the fact that it is seldom taught in churches. Our Lord and Saviour Jesus Christ gave us a clear example of the reasons why many fail to become true disciples. First, what is a disciple? The dictionary definition says this: "A follower or pupil of a teacher, leader, or philosopher." A pupil is one who learns from a teacher, so a true disciple of Jesus Christ is one who would follow His teaching and learn from Him, putting that learning into practice in everyday life.

Consider this passage:

"And it came to pass, that, as they went in the way, a certain man said unto him, Lord, I will follow the withersoever thou goest. And Jesus said unto him, foxes have holes, and birds of the air have nests; but the Son of man hath not where to lay his head. And he said unto another, follow me, But he said, lord suffer me first to go and bury my father. Jesus said unto him, let the dead bury their dead: but go thou and preach the kingdom of God. And another also said, Lord, I will follow thee; but let me first go bid them farewell, which are at home at my house. And Jesus said unto him, No man, having put his hand to the plough, and looking back, is fit for the kingdom of God." (Lk.9:58-62, KJV).

The first man didn't wait to be called but volunteered to follow Jesus wherever He went. Jesus quickly pointed out to him that he hadn't counted the cost of being a disciple. It is very important to count the cost before we start a journey of following Jesus. The twelve disciples of our Lord had left everything. We know Peter was married (Mk.1:30) but he and his friends still left their livelihood to follow Jesus. Matthew left his job as a tax collector to instantly follow Jesus. We may not have to leave our job or family to follow Him, but are we prepared to if He led us that way? We need to count the cost.

The second man in the passage was called by Jesus to follow Him, but he wanted to do something before He obeyed and followed. I've heard of many folk, especially young people, give this kind of excuse. "I want to get my career settled first." "I want to get married first and have a family." There are all kinds of reasons people offer as excuses not to truly follow Jesus, but really there are no valid reasons to put off following Him. He must come first.

The third and final man in the passage also didn't wait to be called, but eagerly assured Jesus that he would follow Him, but after he had gone home to say his farewells fist. We cannot do detours when following Jesus. No good looking back to family, friends, and relationships, because that renders us unfit to serve him fully.

When we come to Jesus and are truly saved, he calls us to follow Him unreservedly. No excuses, putting nothing before Him. He never expects more from you than He Himself was prepared to give. He gave His all upon the cross for you. He left the glories of His Father's house to come to this earth but forsook everything in order to meet the cost of our salvation in full. If we are to follow Him and be His true disciples, nothing or nobody in this world should ever come before serving and being His true disciple.

Pastor Keith Brown
27th May, 2019

Chapter Five

The Carnal Nature Wars Against the Spiritual Nature

HAVE YOU RECENTLY BEEN BORN AGAIN OF THE SPIRIT OF God? You are probably conscious that your conversion experience has armed you with an awareness of a spiritual side to your existence, which you previously had not recognised. Perhaps spirituality was not uppermost in your mind before your conversion and now you enthusiastically long to know Jesus.

I remember vividly when I asked Jesus to come into my life and make a difference. He took over the reins of my life and He forgave my rebellion and sin. Jesus flooded my soul with His peace.

Following my 'born again' experience I was released from the domination of sin which had controlled my actions and thoughts for so long. I was no more under Satan's dominion but translated into the kingdom of God and subsequently living under the authority of God.

My childhood rarely included attending church. I was unfamiliar with Bible stories and so getting to grips with the Bible was an education for me as a young Christian. I dipped into Isaiah in the Old Testament, and I read the Gospels in the New Testament. Christianity was an exciting journey learning about my new faith.

Let me share my experiences further with you.

> It was not long after my conversion before my old nature reared its ugly head! Standing in the dinner queue at school, I bullied a new pupil from her place in front of me. The bullying behaviour by older pupils towards the new and weaker pupils was thought to be acceptable, like an initiation ceremony.
>
> The poor girl barely had time to respond! With one swoop of my hand I slapped her – and hard – across the face! This violent slap involuntarily caused her head to move sideways under the force. My

hand was enflamed where I had just struck her. I stood aghast on seeing the result of my violent action. The pupil's face ballooned with a bright red colour. I was a Christian and very ashamed I was not acting like one, knowing I should behave with kindness and tolerance to others.

In my past before I was a Christian, I had known some pupils feared me. Things were different now as Jesus had forgiven me of my sin at conversion. I sensed immense guilt over this event. For the first time in my life I envisaged how the girl was feeling as a recipient of my uncontrolled anger.

It sounds unbelievable, but it had never come into my mind that my aggressive outbursts were not appropriate. I defended my actions by rationalising I was taking revenge in retaliation to the fate I had received bullying at the hands of the bullies. My revenge was an eye for an eye and a tooth for a tooth! Such violent behaviour was not appropriate for a Christian. I was under a new authority – Christ's authority – since my conversion and having been brought into God's kingdom through Jesus' blood shed on the Cross.

The Holy Spirit spoke to my heart. I experienced the conviction of Jesus. As I stood ashamed in the dinner queue, God impressed upon me that I was a new creation in Christ, and although I had acted impulsively, I could ask Him for forgiveness. This was a new concept for me.

A choice had to be made to let my old nature dominate me or allow the new nature through the spiritual rebirth take control. It was my responsibility to repent to God for the face-slapping incident and apologise to the pupil. This I did.

The face-slapping incident and my behaviour in response to this incident was a predicament I needed to confront. Wasn't I supposed to be dead to sin as the Bible said? If this was correct, which it was, then why had I behaved in this unchristian way?

After receiving salvation at conversion, we have a knowledge that our sin has been cleansed through the blood of Jesus. Furthermore, we know when Jesus died on the Cross, He took us with Him to the Cross, along with our sin, and it was here our old nature died.

When we have an understanding that we were crucified with Christ, a revelation ensues and we see ourselves no longer living as a god on the throne of our life, but we bow to the lordship of Christ.

As the Christian makes spiritual progress, he may feel a pull to take control of the steering wheel of his life, as if the Cross were not enough. In other words, the Christian has a tendency to think, being grateful to God, that he owes Him so much that he must do something for God in return.

There remains an earnestness to know God and welcome His sanctification, but a tug of war ensues between the carnal nature and the spiritual nature.

My reaction towards the girl after the face-slapping incident was remarkable because usually I enjoyed the last word in an argument, and I thought apologising was a failure by backing down. I considered it a huge sign of weakness! I apologised to the pupil for slapping her as she stood in shock whilst I clumsily expressed that she was welcome to resume her position in the queue. I experienced Jesus' forgiveness immediately as a warm and calm feeling of peace which flooded my soul. Only Jesus could have corrected my conduct. I would not have listened to anyone else!

Why have I shared my schooldays experience? In Romans chapter 7 we are shown this very dilemma which I faced in acting contrary to how a Christian ought to. Christians know they should behave Christlike, but the flesh at times coerces us to act quite the opposite. The flesh nature wars against the Christian's 'born again' nature.

> *For I know that in me (that is, in my flesh), nothing good dwells; for to will is present with me, but how to perform what is good I do not find. For the good that I will to do, I do not do; but the evil I will not to do, that I practice.*
>
> Romans 7:18,19

This spiritual struggle is not dissimilar to a tug of war! We want to do the right thing by not sinning, but our carnal nature wars against the spiritual nature within us. The flesh and the spirit are constantly at war!

Christians are conscious of this perplexing dilemma with the carnal fighting the spiritual part within them. This is not unique, and no one is alone in the predicament of the flesh tugging against the spirit, the former tempting us to do wrong and the latter desperately wanting to do right. Temptation comes to all and none of us are exempt.

Listen to the scriptures from the book of Romans on the subject.

The Carnal Nature Wars Against the Spiritual Nature

For I delight in the law of God according to the inward man. But I see another law in my members, warring against the law of my mind, and bringing me into captivity to the law of sin which is in my members. O wretched man that I am! Who shall deliver me from this body of this death?

Romans 7:22-24

Our flesh pressurises us to disobey the laws of God. Our minds are convicted to obey God, and our hearts sincerely want to obey Him, but the flesh nature opposes the new nature born of the Spirit of God. We make decisions and act contrarily to God's commands and, before we know it, get enticed away and lured by the flesh nature! No wonder Romans 7:24 says, "O wretched man that I am!"

The Christian has doubts whether he ever reallyloved doing the will of God, because he now finds it problematic to keep. The carnal nature is active in opposing God's will and so at times he has no desire to follow it; in fact, he finds he cannot.

He questions whether he was even devoted to God in the first place. Confused, he is unsure of his consecration to God and in reckoning himself dead to sin. He knows he has not turned his back on God and ponders in his mind what possibly could be wrong.

Romans 7:18,19 explains that our flesh is unable to do the right thing. It will always oppose the will of God. No good thing can be found in our flesh; even when our desire is to perform what is right, we still practise what is wrong.

Romans 8:1,2 encourages us that we are not under condemnation, because we are "in Christ Jesus" and victory is to be found in "walking according to the Spirit and not the flesh".

There is therefore now no condemnation to those which are in Christ Jesus, who do not walk according to the flesh, but according to the Spirit.

Romans 8:1,2

There is no condemnation for the redeemed of God who walk "according to the Spirit", for what we could not do in ourselves (save ourselves from the condemnation of sin) God achieved through His Son, who took the punishment for our sin. We are born of the Spirit, and if we chose to walk "according to the Spirit" then we are set free from the power and dominion of sin.

We would not be aware of sin, if the law had not revealed it to us.

For apart from the law sin was dead.

Romans 7:8

The law opened our eyes to see its standard on sin, which in ourselves we could not keep. We are under grace and not the law. The law showed us our sin and how far we were from keeping it. Romans 6:14 has been quickened within us, for now we are under the new covenant, a covenant of grace where sin shall not dominate us. When Christ died on the Cross our sinful nature died with Him there. His death for our sin is enough to cover all our sin (Rom.6:14).

The Bible teaches we are "in Christ" (Col.3:3). We are no longer under the old law, which could not save us. We are under the new covenant and the blood of Jesus shed on Calvary has made a way by paying the price for our sin once and for all, and freeing us from the power of sin.

We do not need to struggle against sin, nor should we strive for righteousness in our own strength. There remains a choice, whether we follow our carnal desires or yield to the spiritual nature within us. By faith we have been set free from the "law of sin and death" (Rom.8:2).

The battle between our carnal desires and the spiritual nature vying for dominance, will continue throughout our Christian life, but we are assured of victory through the power of the Cross.

A Christian must not let Satan deceive him into thinking he is not an overcomer. Satan is a defeated foe and heading for the lake of fire (Rev.20:10).

Our spiritual understanding develops when we appreciate God has given us a free will whether we obey Him or not. The decision is ours to either obey the carnal nature, with its selfish and wilful desires, or to follow the Holy Spirit's guidance.

For to be carnally minded is death, but to be spiritually minded is life and peace.

Romans 8:6

We are free to tend towards carnal desires and satisfy its wishes, but as redeemed children of God, purchased by the blood of Jesus, we are called "a chosen generation, a holy nation, His own special people" and as such should live in obedience to God to "proclaim the praises of Him who called you out of darkness into his marvellous light" (1.Pet.4:9).

The Carnal Nature Wars Against the Spiritual Nature

John chapter 15 speaks of the Christian abiding in the vine and explains how Jesus is the vine and we are the branches. We have been adopted into the kingdom of God, and when we sin, we should be quick to repent and so remain abiding in the vine. We can move back into our correct spiritual standing of being positioned in Jesus and continue our walk of faith.

If we sin – and we *will* fall at times – the Bible says we have an advocate, Christ Jesus.

> *If we confess our sins, He is faithful and just to forgive us our sins and to cleanse us from all unrighteousness.*
>
> John 1:9

God has not created mankind like robots but given us a free will. In Genesis, Adam and Eve were given a free will. They were created in the image of God (Gen.1:26) but in the garden of Eden they chose to disobey His command.

We are called and set apart from the world to use our free will to glorify God in living pleasing lives for Him through our actions and meditation (Ps.4:3;19:14).

We can make a determined and obedient effort to walk the way of God's commands by following His precepts in our Christian walk, or flagrantly disregard them.

The flesh and the spirit will war against each other until we are perfected in Christ when He returns and we live with Him for eternity. Here on earth we are changed as He purifies us.

> *But we all, with unveiled face, beholding as in a mirror the glory of the Lord, are being transformed into the same image from glory to glory, just as by the Spirit of the Lord.*
>
> 2 Corinthians 3:18

A Christian should guard his mind and be watchful, not opening his mind to ideologies and philosophies which would draw him away from truth. If he lacks freedom in an area, with an urge to sin and feeling driven, he should seek a mature minister of the gospel for spiritual counsel. Deliverance ministry might be required if involvement in occult practices has taken place, or sexual perversion, or there is substance misuse and addiction.

It is not wrong to be tempted, however our reaction to the temptation is important; we need to endure it. God promises that He will reward the Christian who perseveres in the trial (Jas.1:12).

We could argue in our defence that it is God's fault as He is all-powerful and could prevent us from falling into temptation. Wrong! We should know God does not tempt us to sin, but we are tempted when we are lured away from Him by our own desires (Jas.1:13,14).

We may summarise here by saying that a Christian is aided in his appreciation of his growing faith, when he acknowledges that he must decide how he responds when tempted. There is no doubt this will require much spiritual effort on his part in the battle against temptation.

Our Saviour is near when we are tempted. The Bible promises us that sin will not have dominion over the Christian (1.Cor.10:13).

If we admit our sin, and repent, then the blood of Jesus is sufficient to erase our sin. The blood of Jesus pleads for us before the Father. Our rightful relationship with Jesus is restored in the washing away of our sin through the blood of Jesus shed on the Cross.

This fight between the spirit and the flesh is not a battle for the new Christian alone, but a battle mature Christians face too. Jesus was tempted in the wilderness, and yet He was without sin (Matt.4:1-11).

1. Walking in Victory

There is a part for us to play in our spiritual victory over the tug of war of the flesh warring against the spirit.

> *If then you were risen with Christ, seek those things which are above, where Christ is, sitting at the right hand of God. Set your mind on things above, not on things on the earth. For you died, and your life is hidden with Christ in God.*
>
> *Colossians 3:1-3*

Victory over the carnal nature is made clear in the Bible. We are to seek after spiritual treasure from above, and our affections are not to be tied to the earth (Col.3:2). We are passing through this world and one day will meet our Lord. We must never lose sight of this fact through the highs and lows in life. It is of huge encouragement to remain faithful to God.

There are no shortcuts to a victorious Christian life over the deeds of the flesh, but in daily seeking Bible truths for our edification and by continuing in prayer and communing with God, we have victory. We are inspired to look heavenwards for our succour and strength (Col.3:1).

If our yearnings are fixed on earthly concerns, the danger will be to give fleshly desires room in our affections, where the place of God ought to be first in our heart. When our affections are misplaced, an attitude of rebellion will spiritually disarm us. The consequence of carnal influences will inevitably be a spiritual weakening in our inner man. Such double-mindedness means our affections are not solely upon God and therefore we are susceptible to enticement away from a godly lifestyle. Are you and I susceptible to falling into a trap by giving the devil a foothold?

It is expedient to steadfastly continue in the Bible's commands and statutes. We are children of God and freedom can only be found within its pages. We are set free from our sin and clothed in His righteousness, resulting in us rejoicing in liberty, according to God's word.

Liberty is ours when we obey the word of God, which is a provider of blessing and freedom. This freedom is received when we comply with and obey the written laws of God.

The Bible instructs Christians to consider themselves dead to the carnal man with its passions, desires, and selfish ambition. Our life is no longer our own to do as we please but "hid with Christ in God" (Col.3:3). I believe a window of comprehension is opened which invites the Christian to live uprightly and leads to our liberty, and yet it is only reached through submission to the word of God, as it works in opposition to our fleshly impulses.

2. Dying to Self

We ought to discipline ourselves, by a matter of choice, familiarising ourselves with Bible truth and putting off the deeds of the flesh. Dying to self is a prerequisite of the Christian life.

> *Therefore put to death your members which are on the earth: fornication, uncleanness, passion, evil desire, and covetousness which is idolatry.*
>
> *Colossians 3:5*

We are apt to feel overwhelmed when we think of failing ourselves and God, especially when we fall from God's standards through our weaknesses; but with gratitude we may know, as God guides and quickens us, that our spiritual eyes are opened to view sin how Jesus does: an abomination to God.

The grace and mercy of God is eternal, and because it is, we have an advocate, our Lord Jesus, who, when we sin, is ready to forgive and restore us into our rightful relationship with Himself (1.Jn.1:9).

Let us be wise in our ardour and not lukewarm in the putting to death those sins which would seek to overcome us, but rather choose to walk after the new nature. The Holy Spirit's power is our aid and enabler to accomplish this. Our strength lies in total reliance on His power to overcome sin which is not dependent on self-effort (Col.3:8-10).

Of course, we desire victory over temptation and sin which would trip us up. If we walk in agreement with the commands of God, by putting off our carnal deeds by faith, we will know the power and victory of the Cross. This is a choice as we cannot know victory over sin unless we comply. Our old nature, the unregenerate man, was dealt with on the Cross when Jesus cried, "It is finished." However, we are to purposefully die to the deeds of the flesh (Jn.19:30).

Sin can appear alluring. It is easy for our thoughts to be affected by what we hear, see, and touch, and yet the truth remains in that our sin was defeated on the Cross. Our victorious Christian life has been purchased and secured. There is strength in the Holy Spirit's power to resist temptation when we are choosing the victory of the Cross and view sin as contaminating our lives.

It is not a sin when we are tempted. Our actions dictate the outcome of temptation, and we must understand this and ultimately whether we sow and reap spiritual death or life (Heb.4:15-16).

It is hoped the new Christian will be inspired to walk transparently with God and with his fellow Christians, whose acceptance of him will be a context in which to create a comfortable atmosphere to share any difficulties. The mature believer can assist here with prayer and encouragement.

God does not leave any of us to flounder over our besetting sins. This is true whether we are new in our Christian faith or an established believer. We must know God hears us and will answer when we call out to Him in faith (Heb.2:18; 1.Jn.4).

New Christians are taught to clothe themselves in the new man with its attributes and are encouraged to exhibit the distinctive fruits of the Holy Spirit (Gal.5). This is the direction for all believers who inspire to live victorious lives through the formation of these qualities in their character (Col.3:12-14).

The Bible is the inspired word of God and as such it cannot lie, for it is divinely inspired through men who were moved by the Holy Spirit's unction, and God is the embodiment of truth (2.Tim.3:16,17).

Christians are dressed in robes of righteousness after the image of their Creator. The more a Christian chooses to walk in the new nature, the less he will tend to the flesh nature. He will hate the sin in his life and look upon it with the same repulsion as God.

3. The Devil is an Angel of Light

How does the devil appear to a person? He transforms himself into an angel of light (2.Cor.11:14).

Satan's ploy is to tempt Christians away from serving God by enticing with sinful pleasures. These pleasures can take many forms, but they are always superior in our affections, taking precedence where God should be first in our lives.

When we participate in immoral pleasures, Satan is only too pleased to persuade us to indulge. He will coerce us into installing self first on the throne of our lives. Tempted in this way we develop a spiritual blindness as we take pre-eminence over our destiny when we ought to be relying on the guidance of God (Prov.3:5,6).

We have been bought with a price which is the precious blood of Jesus and we are not to use our wisdom acting independently of God. Satan's aim is to distract us from enthroning Jesus as Lord in our hearts, by replacing Him with the 'I' of self on the throne of our life.

We are not to be ignorant of Satan's devices (2.Cor.2:11). We must be aware of Satan as "an angel of light" (2.Cor.11:14). If we are tempted, we must not be discouraged. God gives us wisdom liberally, which is at our disposal (Jas.1:5).

The Bible says, "Resist the devil and he will flee." (Jas.4:7). We are engaged in a spiritual battle against the wiles and schemes of the devil. We are instructed to be mindful, and watchful of whom we are wrestling against (Eph.6:10-12). Satan does not enjoy the Christian who walks victoriously with God. Satan is poised to fight and oppose the Christian who resists him and engages in spiritual warfare.

We are told to be sober and vigilant against Satan who is like a roaring lion. He is out to devour us (1.Pet.5:8). He comes to "steal, kill and destroy." (Jn.10:10). Let us be wise and alert on our spiritual journey, and do not let it be you whom Satan seeks to disarm and destroy.

Once we discipline ourselves to put off the deeds of the flesh and put on the new man after the image of Christ, a clearer spiritual vision opens whereby God gives us the strength to fight the enemy's attacks.

We are to guard against carnality and not fathom the road ahead by using our carnal wisdom in place of God's wisdom. It is unfeasible to rationalise spiritual truths through our natural reasoning. We need the wisdom of God. His ways are spiritually discerned, and we will not arrive at a conclusion using our intellect (1.Cor.1:19; 2.Cor.1:12; Jas.3:15).

God requires the Christian to walk in humility. We allow an inroad for the enemy when we disregard this. We ought always to dress in our spiritual armour (Eph.6).

Satan is a marvel in causing division amongst Christians, through shifting our focus off God to spiritually weaken us. The mark of such carnality in Christians is observed in their verbal fighting and gossip of each other, instead of fighting Satan, who is the true enemy after our soul and arch-adversary of the Church!

Chapter Six

Spiritual Warriors

IT IS WONDERFUL THAT GOD HAS CHOSEN CHRISTIANS AS spiritual warriors and co-workers with Him in the kingdom of God. A soldier always operates effectively and likewise Christians as warriors for the kingdom should function efficiently too.

We know we are to be alert knowing who our enemy is in the spiritual realm. We need wisdom how to pray and use the sword of the Spirit. It is fundamental for Christians to walk in the Spirit as successful and empowered warriors in spiritual warfare.

We cannot underestimate the importance of equipping ourselves in the armour of God before getting involved in the spiritual battle. Our fight is never against flesh and blood but principalities and powers of wickedness in Satan's kingdom.

Ephesians chapter 6 has much to say on the armour of God. The armour is our spiritual covering in the war against the enemy. Dressed in the armour of God we are equipped in armoury and prepared to fight our adversary.

You may be young in the Christian faith, but God has equipped all Christians to function as effectual warriors. God can use you. Your usefulness as a spiritual warrior is not reliant upon the length of time you have been a Christian, but in understanding the Bible and a quickening in the spirit in understanding Bible passages relating to spiritual warfare.

We ought to see ourselves as Christ does; we are victorious through His death on the Cross and empowered by the Holy Spirit in prayer and for service. This victory against principalities and powers was accomplished when Jesus cried out on the Cross, "It is finished." (Jn.19:30).

The Bible gives clear instruction on the significance of the armour of God and its use if we are to stand against the devil (Eph.6:13).

Ephesians 6:14-16 instructs us to dress ourselves in spiritual armour. We are to put on the girdle, the breastplate, the shoes and to then take up the shield of faith. After this we are instructed, "And take the helmet of salvation and the sword of the Spirit, which is the word of God." (v.17).

The word of God in print wields no power. It is the Spirit which quickens the word of God, and which gives it life. The Spirit takes the written word which in the Greek is called *rhema,* and breathes life into the spoken word. The written word is quickened and wars against the devil, thwarting his tactics and purposes and bringing them to naught.

We put the enemy to flight by disarming him through the power of the Holy Spirit. Ephesians 6:10 tells us to "be strong in the Lord and the power of His might". We cannot fight the enemy through self-effort, or employing our intellect or common sense. The weapons of our warfare are not carnal. We must fight the foe in the spirit realm. When we speak out the truth to the devil, which is the word of God, then the Spirit is moved to act and fight on our behalf. This is our place of refuge and safety.

There is power in prayer and in reading the Bible. The spoken word is alive to assail and thwart the plans and purposes of the enemy. We are called to be victorious children of God, fighting the foe through the power of the Holy Spirit in intercessory prayer and living our Christian lives through the victory of the finished work of the Cross. This is where our victory is found. Ephesians 6:10 shows us how we are successful in defeating the devil by standing "in the power of His might". We are in Christ and it is from this spiritual position we fight our opponent. We become weak and ineffectual when we attempt to fight principalities and powers of darkness in our own strength.

We may conclude from this that we remain strong in spirit in the face of evil through God's power. God's divine authority is available to us when we purpose to dress ourselves in the armour of God.

We may argue, is the armour of God a necessity in order to spiritually stand strong? Is it not enough with the putting off the old nature and putting on the new nature to withstand the devil? Is this not our reasonable obligation as Christians? It is not sufficient; we need a wake-up call because a spiritual battle rages around us!

When a warrior sets out in battle he equips himself by dressing in full armour and is now suitably donned and protected to face his opponent. His will is set on the task ahead to fight his enemy, but his aim must be to win the battle. The Christian warrior should have this same mindset. We should exercise our will in spiritual things, to be empowered and therefore prepared for the battle. We intercede as a strong lion in prayer; our mind is renewed by the word of God. We submit our will to God, and we are quickened within by His Spirit, and are now prepared to fight.

A spiritual battle is taking place, and we cannot act passively unaware of Satan's strategies in this world, when we have our sights set on being powerful and useful warriors of God! We are in danger of falling prey to Satan's deception if we are nonchalant.

The armour of God is available to all Christians, to protect and equip them when facing evil entities which operate in Satan's kingdom and seek to oppose God's authority and assignment here on earth. We should know the purpose of the armour and its effectualness. God wishes to teach His children to rise as spiritual warriors.

Ephesians 6:14-17 discloses the armour a spiritual warrior should don, which is not dissimilar to a Roman soldier's apparel, who, as a prepared warrior, protected and clothed himself with his armoury before going into battle against the enemy. A Roman soldier would never go into battle without his armour in place, suitably equipped and dressed to go into war. There is no difference for us today, who as spiritual soldiers in God's army engage in spiritual warfare.

1. The Belt of Truth and the Breastplate of Righteousness

Stand therefore, having girded your waist with truth, having on the breastplate of righteousness...

Ephesians 6:14

The belt which hung around the waist in the Roman weaponry was vital, because if the belt were not secure the armour would not be held in place. The loin belt is the belt of truth. Christians should read the Bible which is divinely inspired truth and claim the promises of God revealed in the Bible's statutes and commands. The Christian is in effect weakened when he fails to meditate upon God's word.

Christians are spiritually victorious when they wear the breastplate of righteousness, for they are prepared to stand against the ploys of the devil. Christians can fight the enemy efficiently since they are clothed in God's righteousness and armed with His truth which is the word of God. We are clad in the armour of God when we put on the armour by faith. This is our divine protection.

2. Feet Shod and Prepared to Share the Gospel

> *...and having shod your feet with the preparation of the gospel of peace...*
>
> Ephesians 6:15

The Christian who wears the belt of truth, the word of God, and who wears the breastplate of righteousness, must have his feet dressed and ready for the battle. The feet will be feet well shod to share the gospel at every opportune moment.

Our heart ought to be for the salvation of the unsaved and with an urgency to share the good news. If we are donned in our spiritual armoury, we will face the battle without fear and with a boldness from God to disarm whatever weapon the devil throws at us.

3. The Shield of Faith

> *...above all, taking the shield of faith with which you will be able to quench all the fiery darts of the wicked one.*
>
> Ephesians 6:16

What a remarkable promise from God. As fire is quenched when water is poured on the flames, so by faith in God you and I may quench the fiery darts of the enemy. This verse does not say you are able to quench *some* of the fiery darts of the enemy, but *all* the fiery darts. Faith is the key.

Satan's fiery darts are thrown from different directions and it is impossible to gauge when Satan will throw them. Have you sat by an open fire and a spark has leapt from the fire grate whilst you were fanning it into flame? The enemy's fiery darts work in much the same way, by attacking us unawares, and we are singed and burnt by the fiery darts. We must be alert in recognising the enemy's tactics. It is the shield of faith which quenches the devil's fiery darts and no other means can rescue us from Satan's attacks.

4. The Helmet of Salvation

> *And take the helmet of salvation, and the sword of the Spirit, which is the word of God...*
>
> Ephesians 6:17

A Roman soldier would never go into battle with his head uncovered! An uncovered head without wearing the protective helmet would disarm the soldier in battle. He would be open to the enemy's attack and not prepared to fight successfully to win the battle. It was important for a soldier's protection that he wore his helmet. The helmet of salvation which the Christian wears protects his thought life. If the head is not protected, it leaves an entry for the enemy to infiltrate the mind with doubts and fears.

The shield of faith and the helmet of salvation collaborate and work together. With the shield of faith we are able to quench the fiery darts of the enemy, which seek to penetrate and pierce our minds with negative thoughts. The helmet is a covering for our head, but the shield protects our front from the enemy's darts thrown in our direction.

5. Praying Always in the Spirit

> ...praying always with all prayer and supplication in the Spirit, being watchful to this end with all perseverance and supplication for all the saints.
>
> Ephesians 6:18

We stand complete in our position in Christ offering our intercessory prayers to God when we are correctly clad for battle with the full armour in place.

Christians by faith should daily put on the whole armour of God in preparation for the battle and they will be strategically equipped.

Dressed in the armour we are complete to face the spiritual battle. We will be armed and ready against the enemy's wiles.

> For the weapons of our warfare are not carnal but mighty in God for pulling down strongholds.
>
> 2 Corinthians 10:4

We are not to employ our own wisdom which is after the carnal nature, or earthly ideologies, but to trust in the wisdom of God and His mighty weapons to pull down strongholds.

> ...casting down arguments and every high thing that exalts itself against the knowledge of God and bringing every thought into captivity to the obedience of Christ.
>
> 2 Corinthians 10:5

To win the spiritual battle our thoughts must align with the Bible, in what it says about our circumstances and ourselves. We must cast down imaginations and every high thing that tries to exalt itself above the knowledge of God, and which does not marry up with the truth in the Bible. We are to cast them down and discard by faith.

How often do our thoughts wander from God's truth? We imagine dreadful endings to the situations we face. Often, we are worried and perplexed, and we present to God a solution on how to solve our unfavourable circumstances, which are feeble in comparison to God's solution. We resurrect the deeds of the old man out of fear, and when at a loss as to how to solve our problems, we end up losing our way through the spiritual maze of the battlefield!

We are exhorted to bring every thought into captivity to the obedience of Christ. When we allow our thoughts free reign, we enslave ourselves in bondage to the flesh. We will never find answers leaning to our flesh! Our thoughts must be taken captive in line with the Bible.

God has not left us unarmed for our spiritual journey but has given us armoury to withstand all the fiery darts of the enemy. Our part is to wear the armour of God, stay alert and absorb the truth in the Bible by letting it affect our spirit, quoting scripture at the devil and sending him packing.

The battle has already been won in heaven. We have the strength of the greatest warrior on our side, the Lamb of God slain for mankind, who rose victorious from the grave. You and I can be a warrior and not a worrier in the spiritual battles we confront.

God has not left the Christian powerless, but He has given Christians the armour of God to stand tall and fight principalities, powers, and wickedness in high places, in God's power and wisdom and not our own.

Stand tall and fight as a soldier of Christ! You are a Christian warrior and a soldier in God's army.

CHAPTER SEVEN

Living in His Presence

WHAT A GLORIOUS FREEDOM IS OURS WHEN WE WALK IN The Way, enjoying sweet fellowship with Jesus. Those who have tasted of His forgiveness can never deny such a tender encounter with Christ. It is where our worship of God becomes adoration of Him in living to please Him. This happens simply by resting in His presence.

When our minds are renewed by God, the vision we have of ourselves is brought into line with God's perspective. We cast off the deeds of the flesh and by faith we put on the new man. Christians are mindful to conduct their life consistently with the word of God.

> *And do not be conformed to this world, but be transformed by the renewing of your mind, that you may prove what is that good and acceptable and perfect will of God.*
>
> Romans 12:2

"Be not conformed to this world," is a spiritual principle every Christian must purpose to work out in their Christian walk daily if they are to discipline themselves to live in His presence. If we allow ourselves to conform to the rudiments of this world, inevitably our behaviour patterns and thinking will follow the world's standards and morals and not God's.

Before allowing ourselves to be conformed to anything, we must firstly give permission for a process to happen of conformation of a moral standard or ideology into a certain thinking pattern and behaviour type.

There are consequences when a Christian conforms to the world's fashion, which result from acting out of one's decisive choices. If we desire to live in the presence of God, we must make a daily choice not to accept the world's ideologies and fashions which would pressurise us to side with a worldly and carnal system.

We fail to know God's direction in life when we rely on our intellect and fail to hear God speaking to us by His Spirit. Consequences will follow when we do not renew our mind by the word of God.

The Spirit and the mind must work together. We cannot operate spiritually without listening to the Holy Spirit's voice guiding us, ensuring we walk in unison with Him. The Holy Spirit was instrumental in leading us to God, and so we were be born again of the Spirit of God, and He is the same Spirit who prompts us, working out His purposes in our life. We need only to heed His voice. Otherwise we become ineffectual and dull of hearing.

The Bible instructs us to be renewed in our mind, to be continually renewed by the word of God and the Holy Spirit. We must shake off our old ways of doing things according to the pattern of this world. This is a daily walk in the Spirit which requires us to daily resist and deny the flesh. We do not remain static in our Christian walk. We will either progress or go backwards. We should guard our minds and hearts, and not give Satan ground. It is all too easy to be swept along with the tide by not guarding and renewing our minds through appropriating the word of God and obeying the Holy Spirit's quickening within us.

When a Christian lives in God's presence he will delight himself in the word of God. He has tasted of its goodness and is no longer engrossed in the world's ideologies. He despises the weaknesses he sees in himself in comparison to the holy presence of Jesus. His sin appears gross when he is in the presence of holiness, for he now views sin as God views it, as dross which contaminates his spirit.

As an unbeliever he enjoyed his sinful deeds, but now a Christian and born again of the Spirit, the new life of God within him has changed his perspective on sin. He desires purity of heart, imitating his Saviour in his words and actions, to marry with the word of God.

A revelation of God's holiness in prayer and Bible study has become his delight. This soul desires to linger in the ensconce of God's presence. This soul reflects on his obedience to Christ, his service for the kingdom of God and with a transparency of heart. God cannot help but fan a flame within this soul when He sees such contrition and a brokenness of spirit.

Christ longs to birth a contemplative spirit within the Christian, who pines after Christ alone and is loyal. This is our reasonable service we ought to give Him. We cannot be on fire for God without such earnestness, for the contemplative spirit and a devotion to Christ are inextricably intertwined.

God desires that every Christian should be living in His presence. He wants us to experience the truth, "But we all, with an unveiled face beholding as in a mirror the glory of the Lord, are being transformed into the same image from glory to glory, just as by the Spirit of the Lord." (2.Cor.3:18).

We have been delivered and translated out of the kingdom of this world. We must not be charmed by the world's pattern and a love of it. The Bible instructs on this in 1 John 2:15. We are further encouraged in Romans 12:2.

If we take care to nourish our spirit, we will not be sidetracked by worldly ideologies or our analysis on circumstances, but we will receive the wisdom of God in understanding spiritual concepts.

Walking in the Holy Spirit always involves our cooperation. The mind and the Holy Spirit operate in unison, when we bring it into subjection and allow it to align with the Holy Spirit and the Bible's statutes. Our outer man will follow the Holy Spirit's quickening in our spirit, and so we will come to expect His leading.

We are transformed when abiding in His presence, for in the presence of Almighty God we enter through the veil, pressing on into the glory of God; it is here in His glory we are consumed with the holiness of God. We will no longer be persuaded to fall into a pattern of deception in following worldly ideologies.

> *Beware lest anyone cheat you through philosophy and empty deceit, according to human tradition of men, according to the basic principles of the world, and not according to Christ.*
>
> *Colossians 2:8*

We cannot find a solution to problems through phycological analysis or our intellect as the world. Proverbs 3:5,6 assures us that God will lead us if we put Him first and trust Him to guide us explicitly.

We should pay close attention to our spirit, to strengthen it. This is achieved through reading the Bible and by prayer. In listening to the promptings of the Holy Spirit, we will remain close to Him and enjoy a close partnership.

Jesus as Lord of the Christian's Life

We should purpose Jesus to be Lord of our life with an expression as Lord in every area of our life.

God is not to be used flippantly as a slot machine, calling on Him when we get ourselves into a mess and expecting Him to rescue us by snapping our fingers! This is a very unwise attitude to adopt towards God. In fact, God will not answer insincere prayer, but rather chasten us if our heart is stony in our relationship with Him. Jesus deserves more from us than a lukewarm attitude, which will require our obedience in loving Him with our whole heart.

What is the outcome when Jesus is the central figure in a Christian's life? Firstly, there remains a sincere commitment to Jesus in creating a desire to please Him. The difference with the Christian who is serious in making the presence of God his dwelling place, is in his obedience and willingness to embrace daily Christ's forgiveness for sin and to learn from past mistakes.

Secondly, there will be no spiritual blockages hindering him from entering through the veil into the presence of God. A committed Christian will not wilfully grieve the Holy Spirit. His focus and spiritual direction will be to glorify Jesus in useful service for the kingdom of God and to live a holy lifestyle.

When a newly discipled Christian grows in the knowledge of God and abides in His presence, he very soon notices a distinctive lack of interest and attraction to worldly pursuits he once loved, and which work contrary to the laws of God. He has a new joy and freedom in knowing that Christ's love transcends sensual desires.

The more diligence we give to our relationship with Christ, desiring holiness and choosing eternal values as our primary focus, the more we will reap the benefits of a closer walk with God. We will walk in the Spirit and follow His promptings within us, and be in agreement with His will as we read Bible principles. Our mind is renewed by the Holy Spirit when we read God's word and see truth from His perspective. We come to comprehend more fully the perils of walking carnally, which will harm our relationship with God.

To possess a spiritual mind we must set our minds on spiritual things and regard carnal things as leading to our spiritual death (Rom.8:5,6).

On Being Light in a Sinful World

When a Christian abides in the presence of Jesus, his understanding of spiritual things is renewed in the knowledge of God. He is conscious of his purpose, to be set apart for God as light and salt in a dark world.

He longs to be a light illuminating the darkness around him, shining out to the world as a beacon of hope in a sinful world. He will have known a quickening within his spirit, knowing the significance of the Cross in his life, for it is there he has found forgiveness for his sin. The forgiveness he has received is a deep implication of the Cross and results in a walk of holiness, which leads to living an upright and godly lifestyle.

The outworking of a God-fearing life in the Christian is God's responsibility, whilst the Christian's responsibility is to decide to be a carrier of the gospel message, as a citizen of God's kingdom. The committed Christian is set apart for God, and he is a pliable instrument in God's hands possessing a willingness to share the good news of salvation at every opportunity. This Christian is grateful God has rescued him from his sin, having been translated out of darkness into God's light. This Christian wants to shine out his light.

The believer cherishes the fact he has been chosen to be set apart for God's purpose (1.Pet.2:9).

This soul is not bound by legalism. He is free to proclaim the gospel and lives in holiness and exalts the greatness of God through testifying of Christ.

After we hear the gospel message, a window of opportunity has been opened to us. We may respond to its message in two ways. Revelation 3:8 tells us that the offer of salvation is like a door which Jesus has "set before us". It is our choice whether we walk through this door of invitation. Salvation is offered to all mankind to receive salvation. Jesus warns us that the gate is narrow and many refuse to enter the narrow gate, preferring the broad gate "which leads to destruction" (v.13). We read, "Narrow is the gateway," (v.14) and it is "difficult" which "leads to life", and not many find or choose it. A Christian's commitment to Christ extends to serving others and proclaiming the gospel. These are they who have "gone through the narrow gate" (Matt.7:13,14).

A Christian is one who has encountered Jesus and knows he has been freely forgiven of his sin. He exudes compassion for people's needs, both spiritual and material. He speaks about the gospel and how Jesus has changed his life, but his compassion will extend to reaching the community to help with the needs around him.

The Christian is passionate in his witness to see people come to know Jesus and to experience Him, as they have found Him to be true. They are compelled to go out and seek and serve the spiritually lost.

I would suggest Christians whose commitment is to shine as a light in a sinful world are inspired to search out those without a faith and share the hope of salvation and eternal life. This is not a fleeting action. The gospel has affected them, and their perspective is one of effective service in living out the servant heart publicly.

The Apostle Paul was a zealous preacher. An effectual door of service was opened up to him, in the heart of a godless and pagan people. Paul's preaching turned them away from serving idols, to serve the true and living God. The servant heart within Paul was shown in his selfless service for God's kingdom. This can be realised when in Ephesus hungry hearts were eager for the gospel, in response to Paul's preaching and visiting them in their homes.

Paul wrote, "For a great and effective door has opened to me, and there are many adversaries." Paul was aware of the opposition he faced living under house arrest, yet he persisted in continuing to preach the gospel to all who called on him.

So often our faith and zeal to be a witness for Christ wanes. Revelation 3:14-22 exposes the weakness in the Laodicean church who were lukewarm towards spiritual things. The result of lukewarm Christianity is an apathetic compromise of our faith.

This lukewarmness within the Laodicean church may be assigned to the church in today's society. This letter is symptomatic of a token religion, and one driven by emotion, yet superficial and shallow in its commitment to God, and prevalent in this age.

Let us jump out of our comfort zone! Always be prepared to share the gospel at any given time. We have received salvation through the blood shed on Calvary, we have waiting for us an eternal home in heaven, so let's be forthcoming in our witness and defence of the gospel.

> *But sanctify the Lord God in your heart, and be ready always to give a defense to every man who asks you a reason of the hope that is in you, with meekness and fear.*
>
> 1 Peter 3:15

Our enthusiastic and eager method in speaking for Jesus means we will on occasions encounter opposition. It is acceptable to believe in the gospel and speak its message modestly, but some may feel we are not to upset the applecart with an appearance of radicalism!

Of course, being on fire for Jesus will mean different things to different people. If we are loyal to the gospel, a perception of fanaticism should not deter or worry us.

A Christian on fire for Christ will radiate a passion, as a beacon, and a source of light in a sinful world. Nothing will stop him shining for Jesus. He might be seen as fanatical, but it will not phase the Christian.

Our faith and witness for the Lord ought to surpass that of the Laodicean church. Jesus requires our love for Him; in fact, we are to hold Him in high esteem as Lord of our life.

Living in His Presence Requires His Chastening

Christians, when they sin, are quick to repent, for they know they have grieved their Saviour. The Holy Spirit has planted a quest for purity in the obedient soul, who is open to the correction of God. This Christian wants to reflect his Saviour's love in being an authentic witness for Christ (Ps.51:10). His desire is for a holy and steadfast spirit.

Most of us remember our fathers disciplining us, and we honoured them for it. How much more does our heavenly Father need to discipline His children!

> *Now no chastening seems to be joyful for the present, but painful; nevertheless afterward it yields the peaceable fruit of righteousness to those who have been trained by it.*
>
> *Hebrews 12:11*

Our heavenly Father deals with us as sons, but His discipline is necessary to create a yielded spirit in us. Obedience to God's discipline may involve a price, but it puts us on a straight path.

What are the attributes and qualities which God cultivates in the character of those pure in heart, who exclusively seek to live in God's presence?

> *But the fruit of the Spirit is love, joy, peace, longsuffering, kindness, goodness, faithfulness, gentleness, self-control. Against such there is no law.*
>
> *Galatians 5:22*

A well discipled soul leaves the nest as a young bird leaves its mother's nurturing to venture out on its own. As the young bird flies out from its mother's nest, which has been his abode, so the new Christian is encouraged to find his spiritual wings and fly.

The fruits of the Holy Spirit emerge through the process of learning to be obedient to God and in submitting to His discipline through adopting and obeying the commands of God. The seeds of discipline which have been established in the good soil will grow, producing good fruit in the believer's soul and into eternal life. There will also be fruit manifest in souls coming to know Jesus as their personal Saviour.

How this soul delights in his God – and even more now than when he first soared with Jesus into heavenly places knowing the glorious presence of his Lord! It is a delightful state, and the worldly pleasure he left behind cannot compare with the blissful presence of Jesus.

This soul continues to enjoy Jesus' presence and grows in the knowledge and wisdom of God, simultaneously noticing more earnestly his besetting sins which he knows grieve his Saviour. He may ardently grieve over what it cost Jesus to die at Calvary for him, whilst equally pondering on the godly actions he has omitted to do.

In retrospect he knows he should have performed these godly actions, as his desire to be holy in every area of his life is growing. With this quest for holiness there has been birthed an awareness and revelation of Jesus' holiness, soaring his spirit heavenwards in divine rapture and praise of his Saviour. This gives his soul much comfort.

He is apt to remember this place of glory when he falls and commits even a minor sin. This soul feels badly about himself, more so than previously when he had not encountered Jesus' holiness. The contrast between the holiness of his Lord and his sin casts a dark albeit momentary shadow over his emotions. He feels his wretchedness within! The discipline of God is never a painless process, nevertheless this soul will come to recognise that through God's chastising there is birthed a purity within him and sanctification yet unknown to him.

Our innate nature is disobedient and rebellious. We ought to be keenly aware of this. Our disobedience is in need of correction from God. The outcome will be the fruit of a submissive spirit towards God, where humility will be free to mature.

I recall my experience of the indwelling presence of Christ.

> Living away at boarding school, I prayed with friends in the walk-in airing cupboard, amongst our washing hanging from the pipes,

whilst we perched on tuck boxes, filled with fruit tins and biscuits! It was the only place we could pray undisturbed.

What a glorious prayer room the small walk-in airing cupboard became and filled with God's presence!

I desired to be holy as I prayed and worshipped in the airing cupboard. The veil was torn away obscuring my vision to know Jesus, as I entered the presence of God in worship. We spent many days sitting in that sanctuary, praying and worshipping God. It was there I encountered the tender heart of Jesus. Transported into the glory of His holiness, it would have been impossible for me not to be acutely aware of my sin.

Nowadays I am accustomed to God's ability to strip me of those areas where carnality exists on the throne where Christ should reign. Back then it was a painful time under the searchlight of God's correction.

This discipline of God is not incidental. A discomfort will exist in the soul area, which is the seat of the emotions, when God chastens us (Heb.12:11).

In God's searchlight we can acknowledge our discomfort in our emotions through God's correcting us, for there will rise an abandonment of joy in the soul as God searches the heart, which will overshadow any momentary despondency. The procedure of the Lord's correction isn't painless and yet is necessary if the Lord is to "catch us the little foxes that spoil the vines, for our vines have tender grapes" (Song.2:15).

What are the little foxes which seek to spoil the vine in hindering the Christian from living in God's presence? We know foxes plunder the tender young grapes before they have the opportunity to ripen and reach their maturity. The little foxes in our lives are those assailing sins which, like the little foxes, cause us damage.

These sins emerge as 'little' sins, but they are not too dissimilar to the bigger foxes in the damage they cause, and which we will recognise are detrimental to the growth of the vine. Nevertheless, the little foxes do spoil the vine. Sin affects and touches our spirits. Unaware of their damage we forget to pay due consideration to their devastating influence in stunting our spiritual growth; yet we can be corrected by God through the inroad of the little foxes.

The correction of the Lord reminds us of the presence of the little foxes, which are the persistent sins tainting our walk with God. God wants to eradicate the little weeds before they take root and ruin the grapes by contaminating the vine. The grapes referred to in Song of Solomon 2:15 can be used to illustrate the fruits of the Holy Spirit.

God nurtures the fruits of the Spirit within the Christian. He is in the process of eradicating the little foxes which halt the maturity of the fruit on the vine developing; this in turn will produce the fruits of the Spirit to grow and mature (Gal.5:22-24). This Christian will go on to bring forth spiritual fruit with souls saved for the kingdom of God.

What is the benefit of such discipline? The nature of Christ is holiness and He desires His children to be partakers of His holiness and His divine nature, through disciplining us. It is painful for the weeds to be rooted out since they have developed an attachment in the soul. The focus must remain on maturity and holiness of character which will be gained if we continue in persevering with God's correction.

> *Afterwards it yields the peaceable fruit of righteousness to those who have been trained by it.*
>
> Hebrews 12:11

Living in God's presence and knowing His righteousness should consume our soul; we must not allow ourselves to spiritually stagnate, or let a complacent spirit come between us and our relationship with God. God's foremost wish is for our spiritual enlargement.

The glory of God's presence is not only for the Christian's advantage to receive blessings. The Christian's worship necessitates a focus on the adoration of God for His majesty.

It is advisable to come before the throne of God with a godly fear and awe, when we approach Him in prayer, permitting Him to establish faithful worship in our hearts.

The purpose of God's chastising is to work His holiness in us. This is a sanctifying process, alongside the stripping of the deeds of the flesh. This will instil an obedience to God because He alone can reveal the intents and motives of the heart.

> *Now no discipline at the present time seems to be a matter of joy, but of grief; but afterward it yields the peaceable fruit of righteousness to those whom have been exercised by it.*
>
> Hebrews 12:11

This discipline at the time of God's chastening does not produce a joy in us but on the contrary a grief. When we are corrected by our heavenly

Father, we are in the process of learning obedience. The discipline we undergo is painful at the time, but we ought to bear with the sanctifying journey. It is possible to experience His joy in trials although we will know an agony in our soul. We are sure that the "fruits of righteousness" will be outworked in us (Heb.12:11).

In Jeremiah 48:11 we read of Moab who lived a life of ease and had not known hardships, and consequently became "settled on his lees".

> *Moab has been at ease from his youth; and he hath settled on his lees, and hath not been emptied from vessel to vessel; neither hath he gone into captivity; therefore his taste remains in him, and his scent is not changed.*
>
> *Jeremiah 48:11*

The verse here represents those people who have lived a life of comparative ease. Without knowing trials, hardships, or challenges, we cannot mature or grow spiritual muscle. In the process of maturing good wine, the wine is transferred numerous times from one receptacle to another, to prevent the lees from staying at the base. The wine continues to be shifted in this way until the lees which taint the wine's taste have been removed.

We are like the lees; we must be emptied of self to reach maturity. We travel through trials and difficulties and sifted under the searchlight of the Holy Spirit. Journeying through difficult circumstances, we are emptied of self and learn to rely on God's strength alone to get us through our trials. Those people who have never known trials or tribulations have not been emptied of their lees. They look transparent on the top but are not emptied at the base.

If we do not cast off God's correction, this will ensure us embracing God's quest of holiness in our character. The spiritual lessons learnt will be preserved in our soul. The heart will be all the purer worshipping God for who He is and not dwelling in His presence merely to gain a blessing from Him. In this truth God is well pleased. The disciplined Christian is making progress and is growing in holiness.

We must never consider a life of ease in preference to one of hardships and problems. Moab didn't change; he remained passive and he didn't mature because he had never known a sifting through trials by God.

Moab had the same scent, yet his heart had not changed. Have we changed since we received salvation? We lose our original smell at conversion through God's disciplining us and daily living in His Presence,

God's chastening exudes within us His holiness, which is the sweet aroma of Christ. We are learning what it means to live in His presence.

CHAPTER EIGHT

The Power of the Gift of Tongues

THE CHRISTIAN WHO HAS SUBMITTED TO GOD'S CORRECTion usually exhibits an enthusiastic prayer life. The stripping of carnal attitudes and desires induces a capacity of enlarging a believer's spiritual vision. At times he glimpses the Father's heart of holiness and in beholding His glory is transformed to reflect the image of God.

I discovered the necessity of employing the gift of tongues when I engaged in intercessory prayer and spiritual warfare. The gift of tongues opened a new spiritual dimension in my intercessory prayer life, surpassing any limits in prayer.

The gifts of the Holy Spirit, tongues, the interpretation of tongues, and prophecy, are spiritual gifts given to the Church for its edification and encouragement (1.Cor.12:19). The gifts of tongues and the interpretation of tongues should be used in a Christian gathering.

The gift of tongues has many uses; for example, we build ourselves up in prayer when we speak in tongues. We are given to understand that our spirit is strengthened when we pray in tongues.

The gift of speaking in tongues may be implemented in the following ways:

- A Christian who has received this gift will often speak in tongues in his private prayer life, to build himself up spiritually and strengthen himself in the Lord (1.Cor.14:2).
- Tongues can also be spoken in a church gathering.
- The gift of tongues is a sign to the unbeliever (1.Cor.14:22). When the unbeliever hears tongues being spoken, he will recognise that the believer is speaking in a heavenly language. It is a sure sign to the unbeliever that God exists on hearing the tongue spoken out loud.

- When a tongue is spoken in a gathering of believers and interpreted, the purpose is to encourage and build up the faith of believers.

The use of tongues and the interpretation of tongues are spoken of in 1 Corinthians 14:13-16. In church tongues may be used publicly and often in conjunction with the interpretation of tongues, so the hearers can understand and acknowledge the message.

I often use tongues in my private prayers when words are inadequate to express my gratitude towards God. As my heart overflows in worship to God, I find myself singing in the Spirit.

Any believer who is baptised in the Holy Spirit can sing in the Spirit. The believer, by faith, can receive the words in tongues the Holy Spirit gives him. He is able to sing with his understanding in the Spirit and also in tongues, as the Holy Spirit moves within him. Singing in tongues can be used when our own words are inadequate to express our worship and adoration of God, and we sing in the Spirit as He guides us in tongues. The gift of speaking and singing in tongues can be used in a gathering of believers or in our individual devotions to worship God.

I speak in tongues when engaging in spiritual warfare and in prayer against satanic forces operational in the person whom I am interceding for (Eph.6). Here is an example of my intercessory prayer life in my teenage years.

> My boarding school days were behind me, yet I found myself frequently praying for my fellow pupils. More than a year had elapsed since leaving school and I was unaware of their whereabouts or how they were doing. The pupils branched off in different directions geographically to pursue their individual careers. I lost contact with them. My zeal never waned in prayer for my schoolfriends.
>
> One time whilst I was praying, the Lord laid a burden on my heart for a fellow pupil. I came to learn, as on previous occasions, that when an urgency to pray for someone was impressed upon my spirit, I should be obedient to God with the burden He had entrusted me with.
>
> I acknowledged this godly sorrow was from God for He was wanting their salvation. I often wept as I prayed. The sorrow I knew was for their unregenerate state. Groans escaped my throat whilst interceding, which was surely not dissimilar to the pangs of sorrow I knew Jesus felt for this person's soul.

I was unaware of time passing whilst praying as I experienced a lightness in my spirit which followed each victorious breakthrough. It was as if the darkness in Satan's kingdom oppressing the person had receded.

God opened my spiritual eyes as to how He viewed the unregenerate soul with His unconditional love. An awareness tailed this experience with confirmation from God in a deep understanding of the sadness He felt regarding their spiritual state and need of salvation.

I experienced His all-consuming compassion for the lost which was tender and merciful. My part was to cooperate with God on this journey of intercessory prayer, listening to Him for guidance in prayer.

I prayed in tongues for the salvation of those I knew who were lost. I noticed the tongue changed from the one I was accustomed to using when worshipping God for my own spiritual edification. There was an urgency with this new tongue when the Spirit of God prayed through me. The new tongue was more forthright. I sensed God's sadness. The Holy Spirit was battling the spirits of wickedness and principalities and powers as I spoke with the new tongue.

The Bible makes it clear who our enemy is and who it is that opposes us.

> *For we do not wrestle against flesh and blood, but against principalities, against powers, against the rulers of the darkness of this age, against spiritual hosts of wickedness in the heavenly places.*
>
> *Ephesians 6:12*

The Bible's definition of the unbeliever's spiritual blindness is clear:

> *...whose minds the god of this age has blinded, who do not believe, lest the light of the gospel of the glory of Christ, who is the image of God, should shine on them.*
>
> *2 Corinthians 4:4*

There exists a spiritual battle raging in the heavenlies, fighting Satan and his entities. These are evil spirits that oppose the ministering angels sent from God which go before to prepare the way for souls to receive salvation. We are co-workers with God in the spiritual realm, fighting as warriors through intercessory prayer!

> Taking an active role in praying like this was empowering for me, and there was no comparison between my intercessory prayer life and the prayers I heard from some Christians who were accustomed to addressing God in a repetitive way. My experience in prayer was battling against the evil forces in Satan's realm by the power of the Holy Spirit living within me!
>
> I was learning as a teenager to swim in unchartered waters! After each intercessory prayer session in tongues, the intensity of the burden eased. I instinctively knew when to finish praying. It was as if God said, "That is enough intercessory prayer for today."
>
> I continued to intercede in tongues, knowing God would answer my prayers of faith and reveal through the discerning of spirits the barriers which prevented people receiving salvation.
>
> This new way of praying went beyond my own knowledge or understanding. I learnt as I was moved by faith, praying in tongues, and I gradually grasped the evidence God was answering my prayer as I interceded. This brought immense joy in my spirit.
>
> When employing the tongue in spiritual warfare, I recognised it was during prolonged periods of intense battle, and after much conflict against the devil's entities whilst in prayer, that release came and a knowledge in my spirit that Satan's entities were bound and cast out to wait the judgement seat of God.
>
> There have since been numerous occasions when the Holy Spirit has interceded through me against spirits of wickedness and principalities in Satan's kingdom whilst in intercessory prayer. Afterwards I have known intense joy in victory over these entities.

The gift of tongues is vital in spiritual warfare. Tongues enables the Holy Spirit to pray though a believer, for it is the Spirit alone who knows the mind of God.

This intercessory prayer life is always beyond our capability, for when we step out in faith God uses us in spiritual warfare. Christians often remain ineffectual in not fulfilling God's desire for expansion in their prayer life, but God wants more for his children, to be his co-workers in a relationship with Him. What a privilege that Christians are one with God, just as Jesus was one with His Father.

Intercessory prayer through the employment of tongues is a mighty weapon for a Christian.

The Power of the Gift of Tongues

I recall my conversation with a young woman who was homeless. She was sitting cross-legged on the ground, a Bible in her hand, reading, when I stopped to speak with her. I shared briefly my belief in God and how He is alive today, and she replied by asking me to read from the Bible. I began to read from her Bible on the street the story of the Prodigal Son, in Luke chapter 15.

I have discovered a benefit in my private prayer times with the Lord in speaking in tongues, when I am unable to find the words to pray for a particularly difficult circumstance or a person I am interceding for. On this occasion I prayed in tongues for this young woman in my prayer time. I prayed about her openness (which I had noticed when we first met) to read the Bible, and also regarding her homeless state. We met again, and she was open to hear my experience on how God had changed my life, when I had gone through similar circumstances as she was going through.

It took time whilst continuing to pray in tongues. Specifically, I prayed that God would draw this young woman to Himself and also change her state of homelessness.

I continued to meet up with her and minister into her life when she was in the area over many months. A year and a half later, after not seeing her for some time, I bumped into this young woman and she said she had been housed. She asked for a copy of my autobiography *Darkness to Destiny* which she received from me. I shared that I was speaking in a church the same month and she asked if she could come along. In that meeting she gave her life to the lord.

It is a story of twists and turns and ups and downs. The road has not been easy, and she has continued to struggle, having to face the consequence of wrong decisions made due to addiction. I continue to pray in tongues that she will be free from addiction, knowing there is a battle over her life. Satan does not like his victims to go free. I am aware we do not wrestle against flesh and blood but against principalities and powers.

However, when we pray in tongues and allow the Spirit of God to pray through us, intervening in ways we wouldn't imagine or bring about ourselves, we are confident that He will complete a good work in us and in those we meet and are a witness to of the gospel.

How wonderful this is! We often hear of answers to prayer this way after an initial antagonism towards God.

We may incorporate speaking in tongues in our prayer life whilst interceding for those we have evangelised and built links with. It could be colleagues at work, a social setting, relatives, or friends. Sharing our faith is easier when we are at ease in people's company and comfortable speaking of what God has accomplished in our life and how he has changed us. The Holy Spirit prompts us to intercede on their behalf.

Our part in this is to patiently wait on God in intercession and listen to Him speaking to our hearts. The way God leads us in praying will differ from person to person in our private intercessory prayers.

The gift of discerning of spirits is a necessary gift Christians should use when the gifts of the Spirit are in operation because the gifts can be counterfeited by Satan. We must be wise in the discerning of spirits.

The gift of discerning of spirits is a necessary gift in a church meeting or gathering, to discern whether an utterance though a person is from the Holy Spirit or counterfeit. The devil is well able to counterfeit all the gifts of the Holy Spirit. If, for example, a person has previously been involved in the occult or a false religion, this could give an opportunity, an open door, for the demonic to manifest itself though a clairvoyant spirit. In a Christian meeting where the gift of discerning of spirits is absent, there is a danger of counterfeit gifts openly manifesting themselves. This is detrimental to the church, especially when a controlling spirit is in operation. The counterfeit may also operate in a large gathering of believers where it is harder to control.

The gift of tongues is an immensely powerful tool in evangelism. Whilst praying in tongues to myself quietly, I have discovered this permits the Holy Spirit to move mightily and answer powerfully in a situation or person and in ways I could not conceive or imagine. There is a shift in principalities and powers when we use the gift of tongues in intercessory prayer because tongues is the Holy Spirit interceding through us. At the same time, I am listening to the person I am in conversation with.

We do not always know how to pray, and our spiritual understanding can be limited, but in those times, we may launch out in faith by trusting God who knows the mind of the Spirit. Speaking in tongues is an effectual spiritual gift which has sadly been classed as an inferior gift. An inferior and dismissive attitude towards the gift of tongues and an underestimation of the validity of the gift, probably arises from not understanding what is being spoken in tongues.

The gift of tongues is sharp in its execution in answering prayer. I have known physical attack on my person, yet the moment I spoke in tongues, whether in a whisper to God or in a forthright manner out loud, the attack has abruptly ceased.

Do not underestimate the power of speaking in tongues, which is a heavenly language and a gift of the Holy Spirit sent from heaven to us His children.

Christians should speak out the tongue God has given them in prayer. Tongues can build up the believer into a spiritual warrior. A bodybuilder flexes his muscles which are strengthened and enlarged through the rigours of persistent training and likewise we are to flex our spiritual muscles in the use of the gifts of the Spirit, like prophecy in church, tongues in our private prayers and publicly in church, and using the gift of interpretation of tongues to interpret a tongue given by a member of the congregation.

We should remind ourselves when engaging in spiritual warfare and intercessory prayer not to be naïve. We should be alert, knowing the devil is a strong enemy in his attempt to thwart the purposes of God. We are not to bury our heads in the sand but be wise to the devil's deception.

It would be advisable for Christians employed in spiritual warfare and intercessory prayer on behalf of those in bondage to sin, or the occult, whom they may have befriended and shared their faith with, to seek prayer covering from a mature believer in a church and one who has an understanding of demonic activity.

When I was as a teenager, I launched myself into uncharted spiritual waters to help the addicted and marginalised, through an intercessory prayer life. I did not ask for prayer covering from my church, not knowing the value of this in those days. I threw myself into the deep end! I was naïve in my understanding of how vital prayer covering in ministry is for our protection against the enemy.

Through the decades I have come to learn through experience that there were those operating in the demonic realm who desired my downfall, using curses against me and my ministry by the power of Satan. Unbeknown to me at the time, evil entities were working which were in opposition to the Spirit of God as I ministered to the marginalised. We are to be incredibly careful.

We are called to be "wise as serpents and harmless as doves" (Matt.10:16) for Satan is a ruthless opponent.

We as believers have an important part to play in the body of Christ and likewise our giftings are varied and distributed by God in the Church. All of the gifts of the Spirit are significant, and none are inferior when comparing one with another. The Apostle Paul makes a comparison here between the members in our body needing each other so we function properly. He gives this example:

> *If the foot should say, because I am not a hand, I am not of the body...*
>
> 1 Corinthians 12:15

This is true in the body of Christ, and for it to function in a spiritually healthy and productive manner, it is desirous that all believers actively operate in spiritual gifts.

In summing up, we are to be alert and not ignorant of Satan's devices, having a thorough knowledge of the word of God. It is beneficial when in ministry to ask for prayer covering from mature Christians. The gift of the discerning of spirits is essential when we engage in spiritual warfare, and in deliverance ministry when binding and casting out of spiritual entities, and in discerning the gifts of the Spirit. We should be mindful that all the gifts of the Spirit can be counterfeited by Satan.

Never be apprehensive to launch out spiritually into the deep with God. You will be surprised what He will accomplish through you, and it will be beyond your wildest dreams!

Chapter Nine

Growing in the Knowledge of God

THE BELIEVER BEGINS TO GROW IN HIS KNOWLEDGE OF GOD, but God is mindful of pride creeping in at this stage if the soul remains unchecked.

We have already discussed that sin, which had not previously perturbed the Christian, looms as stalactites obscuring his spiritual focus of God, which may cause a sense of unworthiness in the soul.

Christians at this stage are alerted by a divine quickening in their spirit from the Holy Spirit, that it is God who instigates a godly sorrow over their besetting sin. God's aim is to initiate a wholehearted repentance from them. His intention is to rid the soul of besetting sins which have the potential to spiritually cripple him.

We are now going to look at what occurs within the soul to bring about this sanctifying process. When God removes the dross within us, His handling of us may appear ruthless in its removal! This process is not dissimilar to a craftsman at work refining a precious jewel. The dross is discarded, and the jewel is transformed into a diamond of purity and beauty. Likewise, we come to realise in time that God's chipping away at our sin is needful, in order to create a pure vessel and one honed for His use.

This process brings a Christian closer in his love relationship with Jesus. Complacency and an acceptance over sin no longer exist when sin is viewed as an enemy which taints the Christian's soul and spirit. Sin is akin to the invasion of a foreign army.

The Christian's ache inside himself is a longing for purity in the inward man. David the Psalmist possessed this same desire in his life for transparency which was only to be found in a desire for truth.

> *Behold, you desire truth in the inward part,*
> *And in the hidden part you will make me to know wisdom.*
>
> *Psalm 51:6*

Christians at this stage of spiritual maturity often bask in the knowledge they are their Beloved's and He is theirs! They delight in the truth "that I may know Him and the power of His resurrection, and the fellowship of His sufferings, being conformed to His death" (Phil.3:10).

It may be argued that a Christian who has discovered the baptism in the Holy Spirit experiences a capacity to identify more completely with Christ's sufferings. I believe this happens because the baptism in the Holy Spirit foreshadows a spiritual enlargement in a person's spirit. The baptism in the Holy Spirit perpetuates a profound and personal knowledge of Christ as a reality, which exceeds head knowledge about the character of God. These souls 'know' more entirely the "fellowship of His sufferings" (Phil.3:10) outworked in their spirit.

The baptism in the Holy Spirit opens a new spiritual realm to the Christian. His previous spiritual experience was based on obeying God's word in a legalistic way. Without the Holy Spirit illuminating the word of God, it remained a dead letter to him.

Through the Holy Spirit's empowering, the believer is aware of another spiritual dimension in his relationship with Jesus, by a complete and authentic revelation of the fullness of the Holy Spirit as He moves within the believer. The dead letter becomes the living word of God. What a revelation this is to the Christian when it happens to him!

Another aspect of the outworking of the baptism in the Holy Spirit is where the wisdom of God reveals the intentions and motives of the heart. This knowledge leads the believer into a greater awareness and realisation of the stripping away of the carnal deeds of the flesh (Gal.5:24).

This mirrors a tug of war with the flesh striving against God's Spirit within the believer, who should put off the old carnal nature which operates in opposition to spiritual growth. He must accept the way of the Cross which will incorporate features of suffering. If Jesus suffered on earth, the Christian will suffer too.

The difficulties which challenge our faith can accomplish a lasting character change within us in our surrendering to God's will. Growing up in God is never easy! The fruits of the Holy Spirit will flourish in the obedient believer (Gal.5:22).

There is no doubt this is a painful process. The flesh wants to override God's will for the Christian's life, solving his problems independently of God, with a reliance on carnal wisdom to relieve the soul of the emotional torment in the trial. The flesh must learn to submit to God in the fiery trial and this soul must embrace identifying with Christ's sufferings; then he will learn the spiritual lesson in 1 Peter 4:12-15.

The Christian is aware that the procedure of weaning from the milk of the word onto spiritual meat is not a painless one! If the believer perseveres in prayer, putting off the old nature and putting on the new nature by faith, God's righteousness will be manifest in him, and he will exhibit the fruits of the Holy Spirit revealed in godly character (Eph.4:22-24).

We read of this weaning off the spiritual milk onto the meat of the word in the book *The Dark Night of the Soul* by St John of the Cross:

> *Souls begin to enter this dark night when God draws them forth from the state of beginners ... and begins to set them in the state of progressives ... It must be known, then, that the soul, after it has been definitely converted to the service of God, is, as a rule, spiritually nurtured and caressed by God, even as is the tender child by its loving mother, who warms it with the heat of her bosom and nurtures it with sweet milk and soft and pleasant food, and carries it and caresses it in her arms; but, as the child grows bigger, the mother gradually ceases caressing it, and, hiding her tender love, puts bitter aloes upon her sweet breast, sets down the child from her arms and makes it walk upon its feet, so that it may lose the habits of a child and betake itself to more important and substantial occupations. The loving mother is like the grace of God, for, as soon as the soul is regenerated by its new warmth and fervour for the service of God, He treats it in the same way; He makes it to find spiritual milk, sweet and delectable, in all the things of God, without any labour of its own, and also great pleasure in spiritual exercises, for here God is giving to it the breast of His tender love, even as to a tender child.*

The fruits of the Spirit in Galatians 5:22-24 are cultivated within us through growth in the spiritual tug of war between the flesh and the regenerated spirit within the Christian. In submitting to the Holy Spirit's correction, God can create holiness in the character of a person. Chewing on the meat of the word, we gain spiritual sustenance and leave behind us the milk of the word.

This Christian is relieved he has survived the ordeal of the fiery trial! He notices positive changes in his thought life. His reliance is now on the promises of God in the trial, not allowing negative emotions to dictate his actions, which is indicative of this spiritual growth and change in his behaviour.

This soul is often unaware he is growing in God, but nevertheless the promises of God are being outworked in his life and preserved in his soul. Christians are instructed to put away worldly ways and ideologies which they were accustomed with, and which they ran their lives by (Col.4:22).

This believer is starting to lean on the promises of God through adversity as he learns to walk in the Holy Spirit. When he encounters a similar spiritual battle, he may draw on the promises of God which have proved faithful and which saw him though a previous trial. These promises of God are those which he has stood on by faith in the trial and which have brought him through to a place of victory. These truths are now preserved in his soul. His faith in the promises of God in conjunction with the quickening of the Holy Spirit within him has wrought a change in his character.

This soul has obtained and reached a spiritual plateau. He is pleased to have attained such heights, where pride is largely absent; for he rightly perceives it is God's guidance and not his own wisdom which has brought him thus far through difficulties.

The significance of the Holy Spirit's work in this believer's life is evident with the wisdom of God operational in his life and God's dealings with him in a purifying and refining work through the trial.

Job was a righteous man in the Old Testament, who came to the point where he could say, "I have heard of you by the hearing of the ear but now my eye sees You." (Job.42:5). He came to understand God's dealings with him in his grief, loss, and sickness which were higher than his own thoughts and perception of his circumstance. When Job cried, "My eye sees you," this signified that he saw his hardships from God's perspective and in a new light, no longer through the lens of his friends' poor advice. God's wisdom transcended Job's limited understanding on his adversity. Job possessed a clearer insight into God's dealings with mankind but also into God's dealings with him. Understanding that "my eye sees" would require a divine revelation on who God was in his majesty, omnipotence, and holiness, which went beyond hearing about Him. Job's "seeing" affected the course of his life profoundly. He understood God's sovereignty in his life. Nothing had happened by chance to him, for God's thoughts and ways were higher than his thoughts and ways.

Like Job's experience of grief and being perplexed in his trials, so the Christian is embarking on a new spiritual journey through his trials. This Christian is learning the spiritual lesson of putting off the old man.

> *Be not conformed to this world, but be ye transformed by the renewing of your mind.*
>
> Romans 12:2 (KJV)

He is grasping little by little the sanctifying process he must journey in the renewing of his mind, which will continue a lifetime.

The Withdrawing of His Presence

The withdrawal of God's presence is a painful lesson for the Christian and one which does not always denote he is in a backslidden state. It could be a contributory factor but is not the only reason why a believer goes through periods of the absence in his senses of the closeness of Jesus' presence. For the Christian who has entered into the fullness of God and has stirred up "the gift of God which is in you through the laying on of my hands" (2.Tim.1:6), this is a bitter pill to swallow.

Indeed, we are encouraged to continually seek to be filled with the Holy Spirit. Christians must take heart. The withdrawing of God's presence is not by accident, but a necessary nurturing and one designed by God to strengthen our faith, intended to bring us into spiritual maturity.

We can say, as David the psalmist, "How long, O Lord? Will You forget me forever?" (Ps.13:1), "Lord, why do you cast off my soul? Why do you hide Your face from me?" (Ps.88:14).

With the prolonged absence of the Lord's presence, the Christian can feel bereft of God's love in his soul area, with a real anguish and loss, and since mankind was created for fellowship with God, the soul pines for a connection with the Creator.

The Psalmist David knew the same pain! "You hid Your face, and I was troubled." (Ps.30:7).

This Christian is weaned off his reliance on God's presence, but a witness remains within his spirit that he is born again of the Spirit of God and that God *is* "Immanuel, which is translated, God with us" (Matt.1:23). God's word remains true when feelings of the presence of God are absent.

If the Christian is not taken off guard spiritually with the withdrawal of God's presence, he may focus on familiarising himself with Bible promises and statutes which will confirm his spiritual position in Christ.

He will not leave you nor forsake you.

Deuteronomy 31:6 (cp. Hebrews 13:5)

The certainty and security of God's word is not dependent on fluctuating feelings whilst travelling through the process of this spiritual weaning.

There is a purpose which God will reveal to the Christian journeying this road. God has a plan to enlarge the spiritual vision and we should continue to trust Him during the absence of His presence. Our feelings are fickle, but God's word is the ultimate truth.

He who trusts in his own heart is a fool, but whosoever walks wisely will be delivered.

Proverbs 28:26

It is significant how we chose to walk in the wisdom of God during this new spiritual phase. I would suggest a Christian discipled soon after his conversion is less likely to flounder when trials and testing come. We explored this subject in Chapter 1. This is because our faith will stand strong in adversity when roots are planted deeply in the good soil. Our faith will increase despite a lack of God's presence in this spiritual stage (2.Col.6:7). The Bible encourages and reminds us, "For we walk by faith, not by sight." (2.Cor.5:7).

If the Christian draws on the resources found in the Bible, he will refrain from doublemindedness in his walk, which always creates an instability in spiritual growth (Jas.5:7,8).

Jesus leads the Christian to rely on the Bible as his guide and not rely on fluctuating emotions. The believer will reach maturity of faith and edification.

...that you were enriched in everything by Him in all utterance and all knowledge, even as the testimony of Christ was confirmed in you.

1 Corinthians 1:5

This stage of growth can be puzzling to Christians who rightfully argue they are to be continually filled with God's presence as Spirit-filled

Growing in the Knowledge of God

believers, and yet the reality is one of experiencing an absence of God's nearness. They often feel God has abandoned them.

We cannot fathom the way God hones us to be holy by our natural reasonings. God's ways are spiritually discerned and can only be understood and revealed in our spirit through a divine revelation.

The way forward in the trial of our faith is in surrendering our will unreservedly to God when the journey is void of light, and trusting Him patiently along this new path (Deut.33:27; Ps.34:17; Is.30:15).

> I remember as a young Christian, and not long into my spiritual journey, I was aware of Jesus' presence in whatever task I undertook and wherever I went.
>
> I was away from home at Easter time attending a Christian celebration with my fellow Christians. I was fifteen years old. A group of Christians was meeting in a chapel. I joined in enthusiastically with the crowds gathered, but unusually for me I was mourning the loss of a feeling of God's presence within me.
>
> I was accustomed to entering beyond the veil and worshipping Jesus in the beauty of His holiness, which I experienced as I worshipped. The jubilant outpouring of worship, dancing, and tambourines raised before the Lord was conducted with a freedom in the Holy Spirit I had not previously encountered.
>
> I longed for a word from God that He still cared for me, even with the withdrawal of His presence. I figured I had committed the unforgivable sin!
>
> A while passed and then I saw a woman walk towards me. She stood awkwardly in between my chair and the one in front. I lifted my tear-stained face and found myself looking into the eyes of Aunty May, as she was affectionately called. An elderly and mature Christian, she was full of wisdom. I had previously lodged in her cottage on visits to this fellowship.
>
> Aunty May gently laid her hands on my head and prophesied. I did not pay much attention to the worship around me, for all I could hear were Aunty May's words of comfort from my heavenly Father's heart to mine. My thoughts of Jesus' abandonment of me melted. Jesus had felt so far away and yet how could God forget me? The Bible says of Christians, "See, I have inscribed you on the palms of My hands." (Is.49:16).

> Aunty May prophesied, "I have not forgotten you." Much of the prophecy went over my head, except her words to me, "You will lead many people to God of your own age." She continued speaking prophetic words over my life. The sadness I felt left me. I experienced the comforting presence of Jesus once more.
>
> Aunty May's prophetic words were fulfilled over my life. I went on to lead my fellow pupils to Jesus whilst at boarding school.
>
> I do not recall learning a spiritual lesson back then on the absence of God's presence. I just remember hearing those comforting words from Aunty May. I was overjoyed that Jesus' presence had returned whilst I worshipped God! I was grateful He had not deserted me! My comprehension on the ways of God were immature in those days.

I write of my experience of the withdrawal of the presence of God, because it is beneficial when Christians journey through a similar spiritual stage to know the importance of speaking with a mature believer, one who can guide them through this trial of their faith.

We must consider when embarking on this new journey to guard the spirit against any root of bitterness towards God. This can ensue when we have doubts on God's leading with the withdrawing His presence; and it is too easy to question whether our past spiritual experiences meant we were on the right track or even whether they were valid. We are taught to be prudent and must refuse to allow a bitterness to taint our spirit (Heb.12:15).

This is a spiritual stage that we must walk through and we are to trust God implicitly through it, for this road is not comparable with past spiritual experiences and revelations.

We are called not to compare the benchmark of holiness in our life with that of fellow Christians. Our benchmark is only comparable with God's standard of holiness written in His word (2.Cor.19:12).

It is not wise to analyse this spiritual stage with the withdrawal of God's presence. Satan will tempt the Christian to reason that he has committed the unforgiveable sin and by so doing offended God, causing Him to turn His back. I possessed these same thoughts when, as a young Christian, I travelled this spiritual road with the withdrawal of God's presence. This is a lie from the pit of hell.

It is during this spiritual stage that Satan takes advantage by instilling negative thoughts and doubts as to why God would allow this to happen. The devil uses this ploy against a Christian to deter him from focusing

Growing in the Knowledge of God

on Bible promises and truths, which would surely advise him with wisdom he so dearly craves.

This believer's spiritual understanding is limited, and fathoming his spiritual walk from a tunnelled perspective does not help him. His negative attitude is revealed in his blind spiritual state on Bible truth, and furthermore evidenced in an unwillingness to receive instruction from the Holy Spirit (Prov.8:33; Jer.6:10;7:23,24). He is not as yet able to accept and truly desire God's illumination, as he feels God has abandoned him. This Christian is in danger of missing God's instruction if he does not cast his emotions aside.

Satan plants negative thoughts and lies as seeds. A Christian must know the battle is spiritual, against principalities and powers, and not a carnal war (Jn.8:44; 2.Cor.10:3-5).

The secret is in knowing God's sovereignty and declaring the new covenant's promises. The believer is a new creature in Christ (2.Cor.5:17). Their spiritual standing is positioned, knowing they are 'in Christ' and not veering towards double mindedness when encountering trials. God is teaching these Christians of His desire to refine them. They should trust in His word implicitly whilst journeying through the dark, despite a void and lack of God's presence. They will be empowered by the Holy Spirit through this weaning process, which is not dissimilar to a child's weaning off milk and learning to chew on meat (1.Cor.3:1,2). They will learn in time to chew on spiritual meat if they continue with this necessary procedure of spiritual weaning.

This Christian can be courageous and remind himself of the Bible's promise to him which states his spiritual position is planted securely on the firm foundation, which is Jesus Christ. He is walking uprightly with God during times of the withdrawal of God's presence.

He should be encouraged to walk this journey conducted by faith and not by sight. He has not fallen out of favour with God. If he is walking closely with God, then the withdrawing of God's presence does not denote sin in his life. God is not displeased with him.

During this trial, the believer will undoubtedly grow in faith, without placing undue emphasis on an awareness of God's presence, but in worshipping God for *who* He is, as sovereign God over his life (1.Chr.16:29; Jn.4:23,24).

The believer will develop an awe of God as the Holy Spirit teaches him that he can do nothing without God. This extends even to his sincere worship of God. In this trial of his faith he will know enormous inadequacy and feel out of his depth in his soul area, but he must take time to absorb in his spirit that the origin of his strength is in God alone.

This Christian is presently at the stage of spiritual maturity where he reasons he is correct in summoning God's presence when he so wishes! This will of course mean he becomes distraught with the lack of God's presence.

Christian maturity comprises worshipping God when at times we do not have a sense of His presence with us. We are called to worship God for who He is. He is the Lord of heaven and earth and we should not only worship Him to receive the blessings which He bestows on us. If God decides to grace us with His presence, so be it, and if not, we must be fine with that also.

During this stage, it is imperative the Christian guards against pride (Jas.4:6; Prov.16:18; 1.Cor.10:12; Prov.13:10; 1.Pet.5:5) and practises humility.

The Christian may recall previous times of refreshing in the Lord's presence, and yet he is persisting in this spiritually dry wilderness, which is not unlike a barren land, and not dissimilar in nature to an endurance test! He may reminisce on his faithfulness to God and recall his obedience and delight in sharing the gospel. It is not uncommon for the soul to indulge in self-pity when rationalising what is happening to him.

Envy and a jealous spirit are prone to creep into the heart when he observes his fellow Christians enjoying the blessings which he thinks he has lost forever and is missing out on (Jas.3:14-16; Prov.14:30; Gal.5:19,26; 1.Cor.13:4).

"Why have you forsaken me?" this soul cries out to God in his lament, just as Jesus did (Ps.22:2; Matt.2:46). "I walked with you. I shared the gospel. I walked closely with you!" this Christian may cry out to God. Pride is all too apparent in this believer, but sadly as yet he has not received enlightenment on his spiritual state; and because of self-pity he tends to lack a receptive and teachable spirit on the Lord's instruction.

This Christian is viewing his current situation from his own viewpoint. He is not discerning that God is working all things out for his good (Rom.8:28). He lacks discernment and fails to currently see the bigger picture, which thankfully God does!

We need to recognise that the employment of spiritual gifts does not equate to spiritual maturity. A babe in Christ who has obtained the gifts of the Holy Spirit will come to see how God is wanting to form a godly character and mould him into a spiritual vessel, in collaboration with the spiritual gifts (1.Cor.12).

God is weaning this Christian off a dependency upon God's presence, so that his faith will not rest on feelings but on the word of God.

> *So then faith comes by hearing and hearing by the word of God.*
>
> Romans 10:17

By studying and meditating on God's word our faith matures.

A Christian must learn to worship and serve God apart from receiving blessings from Him,

> *God is Spirit, and those who worship Him must worship in spirit and truth.*
>
> John 4:24

This is a hard lesson for this Christian, who is like a babe coming to his mother for sustenance. It is biblically correct a Christian should desire to be filled with the Spirit of God. The withdrawing of God's presence is a hard lesson for a Christian to comprehend when his present spiritual wilderness condition appears a contradiction to his experience of God's dealings with him thus far! There is no co comparison between his spiritual state before this trial and the road he is now embarking on.

He is travelling a different journey to his fellow Christians, as believers travel through different spiritual stages at different points of their lives. It is a journey which includes the chastening of the Lord and this spiritual stage is paramount for this Christian if he is to grow in his relationship with God. This road is especially tailored for him by God (Heb.12:7-11). With the withdrawal of God's presence this soul may be aware of pride creeping in, which he had not noticed when experiencing the glory times of blessing!

If God had left this believer on the mountaintop and he had stayed there, he would have missed many valuable lessons. God loves his soul too much to leave him there! This soul will come to understand this later, but for now he remains perplexed.

In journeying through the wilderness experience the believer recognises the sins of envy and pride poking their heads up like weeds in the grass! It was easy to die to the deeds of the flesh in the past when he felt the Lord's presence near him! Now he must make every effort to die to the carnal deeds and allow the word of God to dwell richly within him.

He may not feel God's presence, but nevertheless he is spiritually growing.

If this believer perseveres by trusting in God's faithfulness, his spiritual vision will instead focus on the awe and fear of God (Prov.14:27; Ps.111:10).

His spiritual longing for God's presence will be met and satisfied once more when his faith is not reliant or dependent on chasing a feeling of the nearness of God.

His past worship which he cherished was in part selfish. Its purpose largely existed to entertain approval from God and seek blessings from Him. But it is now transformed and is sanctified by a purer vison of God's holiness. The believer's focus is to glorify God through worship now and he is transformed by this self-denial.

In his adoration of God, he pours his love and gratitude upon his God, for what has been born within him is a reverential fear and awe of God. The withdrawal of God's presence felt in his soul has now taught him the true meaning of pure worship and what godly fear of the Lord truly is!

Here this soul grasps the wisdom of God, that, "He who abides in Me, and I in him, bears much fruit; for without Me you can do nothing." (Jn.15:5). This comprises worshipping God in "spirit and in truth." (Jn.4:24).

This soul is starting to die to self-reliance and God is well pleased with this believer.

Chapter Ten

The Dark Nights of the Soul and the Spirit

A wounded spirit, who can bear?

Proverbs 18:14

THIS DARK NIGHT OF THE SOUL EMBODIES THE WOUNDED spirit.

My experience in travelling through the dark night of the soul and the dark night of the spirit was an intense desire for God's purification in my life. I wanted God to create in me a holy vessel. I was ardent to become someone He could use for His kingdom in a larger way. This would involve the development of my character. This would happen through suffering and the Holy Spirit's enabling and strengthening to go on to produce the fruits of the Spirit within me.

This purification process continues over the lifetime of all Christians, and none will reach a state of purification overnight! Indeed, we will not be completely like Jesus until we leave our mortal bodies and we see Him face to face in glory. "...when Christ appears, we shall be like Him..." (1.Jn.3:2).

Identifying with Jesus' death on the Cross, I understood Jesus was desirous to purify me and this was revealed in a revelation in my spirit. I understood my sufferings would change me and that I would eventually cherish this dark and obscure road to find "treasurers in darkness" (Is.45:3). God had prepared the dark night of the soul for my spiritual growth. It was no accident I was journeying this road which was void of any light.

I understood in an exceedingly small way Jesus' experience of anguish in His spirit which he endured in the Garden of Gethsemane, when he cried, "If it be possible take this cup from me." (Matt.26:39).

I wanted my cup to pass away from me. This dark night was too perilous to even contemplate. It was a road filled with unimaginable pain, but I could not close my mind to it.

Journeying through this unusual dark night meant every sense in my faculties and the spiritual revelations revealed to me through the Holy Spirit appeared dead and buried, and even my physical strength had broken down. It was as if I had fallen into a devilish pit in body, mind, and spirit.

Before I explore the characteristics of the dark night of the soul, I will share the spiritual road that 'beginners' travel by using an illustration and extracts from St John of the Cross' account, in his book *The Dark Night of the Soul*. St John backs up the experience of the dark night of the soul with biblical references, and his deep insight will hopefully shed light and wisdom on this subject, helping us to spot if we ourselves are travelling this road.

These "beginners", as St John refers to them, may have been committed followers of Christ for many years, enjoying encounters with God and studying the Bible enthusiastically. These will be mature and sanctified Christians. They probably would not consider themselves as beginners in their understanding of spiritual wisdom, revelation, and knowledge of God.

The deception of Satan is such that we tend to misunderstand the true meaning of spiritual maturity. We arrive at a conclusion from our carnal reasoning and our intellect, comparing past spiritual experience with that of the present. This is because the soul area has not yet travelled the dark night and, so ingrained are imperfections, the Christian does not understand the wisdom of God in this season. His spiritual eyes have not obtained illumination from God on the true condition of his soul.

The Imperfections of Beginners

St John expands on the imperfections of beginners, who may have been committed Christians for years or not long travelled the Christian path. It is important to have a comprehension of the characteristics of the beginner's spiritual understanding and experience, which we will delve into first, because this will allow us a deeper comprehension of the darkness of the 'dark night of the soul' experience.

This road of the dark night of the soul is unusual and certainly an obscure path, which God does not lead many souls to travel, according to St John of the Cross. He describes this spiritual road as an "advanced one".

Dealing with the "imperfections of beginners", he writes that God is desirous to "move them on" and for them to progress spiritually. This is true of those souls that are eager for God and are already "contemplatives", those who delight in meditating on God's word and take enjoyment in hearing from Him and waiting in His presence.

The Beginner and His Contemplative State

God's desire for these beginners is their spiritual growth. He desires to move them on from their contemplative state, so they may "arrive at the state of the perfect, which is divine union of the soul with God". One way for us to understand this spiritual progression is by recognising the characteristics of spiritual beginners.

As a spiritual beginner, I longed to be holy and I desired purification in all manner of my walk with God. God graciously enabled me to see my weaknesses, which led me to earnestly desire to be rid of imperfections. It was His direction for my life and His will which led me to journey into the dark night of the soul.

I was desirous, as St John of the Cross aptly describes, for my soul to be "strengthened and confirmed in all goodness" (1.Pet.5:10). Not only this, but my soul was ready to know "the inestimable delights of the love of God". The worst spiritual state for me would have been stagnation in my walk with God.

St John acknowledges the role of God in the beginner as a nurturer of the soul, just as a mother nurtures her child. However, there comes a time when, after a baby gains sustenance from the breast milk, he must grow, and so he is weaned off his mother's milk onto solid food. We discussed this weaning process in the previous chapter.

Likewise, for the beginner in Christ to move onto the meat of the word, this weaning process has to happen. St John explains:

> *The loving mother is a picture of God's grace, in that as soon as the soul is reborn by the Spirit of God and acquires a new warmth and love for God's service, God acts just like a mother. This new-born child of God tastes all the goodness of the 'spiritual milk, in all godly things'.*

He does not have to work to obtain it. St John endorses this and the "great delights in spiritual exercises" which God allows this soul to taste and enjoy. This soul is nurtured as a babe in its mother's arms.

The Seven Deadly Sins and God's Weaning Through Dryness and Inner Darkness

St John of The Cross emphasises a tendency characteristic in the soul's behaviour, whereby the beginner's motivation towards spiritual things largely originates from blessings they receive from God because they derive much pleasure from it. They find consolation in fasts, and sacraments, but their motives in these spiritual exercises have not been purified. Furthermore, the weakness in virtue in these souls is their focus to work for the pleasure gained from such spiritual activity.

Their weaknesses are seen in the seven deadly sins which describes their spiritual state, and St John reiterates that "the dark night of the soul brings so many blessings with it" as this beginner is purified and sanctified from all the soul's flaws.

St John lists the seven deadly sins: pride, spiritual avarice, lust, anger, spiritual gluttony, spiritual envy, and sloth. He describes how much these beginners need to enter the advanced stage "to make spiritual progress" (Prov.6:16-19).

> *There he weans them from the breasts of indulgent spiritual pleasure and gives them dryness and inner darkness. He takes from them everything that is irrelevant and puerile. In a very different way, he enables them to find goodness. For no matter how carefully the beginner practises dying to self he will nowhere near succeed until God works in him through the means of purification of the dark night.*

The Three Signs One is Entering the Dark Night

St John of the Cross identifies clear signs that indicate a person is embarking upon this dark night.

We will look at the various reasons for spiritual dryness a Christian will encounter. The Christian with apathy towards God cares little about his spiritual growth and has a lack of desire to walk in the ways of God (Rev.3:15-16; Jn.5:39-40).

There is also a spiritual dryness Christians go through which occurs when we are physically unwell. We are less able to pray and read God's word, because of our debility. Similarly spiritual dryness may also happen to the mentally ill, with an inability to comprehend God and His dealings with them.

The dark night of the soul St John talks about is different and unique to the other spiritual dryness we have discussed here. The spiritual dryness in the spirit of a person occurs during the sanctifying process of carnal desires, which seek to dominate our emotions, motives and actions instead of the Spirit. The spiritual dryness felt in this dark night is distinct for the following reasons. It is present when God is seeking to create within the Christian a deeper work of purification and it is not happening because of a physical reason or apathy towards God. Going through this dark night is a painful process when the 'soulish' in us is being purified.

There are three signs which he suggests are indicative of a soul approaching this dark night of the soul.

The First Sign

Firstly, the soul embarking on this new dark night experiences a distinct lack of gratification or satisfaction from creation or things generally in the world, and no comfort in spiritual things either (Lam.3:2,8). God has designed this soul to find distaste in the things of God and life itself because He wishes to "dry it out and purify it from its physical appetites". He will not allow this soul to find delight or satisfaction in anything.

We can conclude this "dryness and flavourless state" is not the result from recent sin or this person's flaws. If it were so, this soul would find pleasure in his sin and things "other than God". When a soul sets his mind and emotions to enjoy a pleasure, and a distinct lack of pleasure in life exists, that can be an indicator (although not a guarantee – we must consider both the physical and the spiritual health of a person). This a new dark night of the soul which they are journeying.

The Second Sign

A sign of purification for this soul in that although "his mind is frequently centred on God" this period is of great concern to him, where "he believes that he is not serving God, but rather backsliding". This soul has come to this conclusion because he has "no pleasure in the things of God". This is different from being lukewarm and the dryness which occurs when a person has little concern for the things of God. This second sign of entering the dark night occurs when the Christian "takes no *pleasure* in things of God".

This soul is passionate in His spiritual walk with God, and is in distress over his spiritual dryness, which does not originate from a physical weakness or a lukewarm spiritual state – if it were so, he would not care for the things of God.

Lukewarmness is characterised by a neglect in the things of God, such as praying to God and reading the Bible, and keeping short accounts with Him in confessing shortcomings and sin in daily repentance. Some are weak in their will and spiritually weak in their spirit and their resolve to follow Christ and keep His commands.

> My experience on entering this dark night was one of worry, in which I tried to analyse the stale dryness of my spiritual state. I was so enthusiastic for the things of God, but the dryness was now so present in this new dark night.
>
> I found no satisfaction in the things of God and this troubled me deeply in thinking I was backsliding. Life itself was a chore to be endured, and this, coupled with a lack of pleasure in life in general, when before I had walked with God closely, caused my spiritually dry state to be unbearable.
>
> Part of the horror of this dark night was because of my lack of knowledge about it. I was bewildered as to why God should permit me to journey through such an arid, dry spiritual land, where no comfort or solace could be found. I had no idea God was preparing me through this dark night for a new spiritual level of purification, which only this dark night could accomplish within me.

The soul travelling through this dark night, at this particular stage of his journey, hankers after the blessings he has known because it is a familiar path to him and one where "the spiritual palate has become used to the other delightful tastes on which it still centres its attention".

> I missed my close relationship with Jesus, when the spiritual delights I had basked in and loved had been so exquisitely a blessing to my soul. These spiritual delights included the closeness of God's presence, and a revelation of His holiness as I entered the glory of His presence, with visions and revelations.
>
> Now I was embarking on a new path which was one of spiritual dryness. The dryness in the dark night of the soul was so much drier and emptier than any dryness I had previously encountered. My spiritual palate had difficulty in adjusting, as mountaineers

acclimatising to a higher altitude; likewise, my soul and senses cried out in agony at the presumption that God was abandoning me!

The truth remains that the spirit within the soul travelling through this dark night of the spirit is very much active, although it does not appear to be so to the Christian who is in great distress due to his dry spiritual state and lack of pleasure in life. "The spiritual dryness may be accentuated by a depressive state of mind." The "unspiritual part of the soul is at low ebb", because nothing can satisfy it.

The Third Sign

The third sign is how God speaks to the contemplative soul. There is an inability to meditate upon God's word as previously. "God is no longer communicating through the soul through its mind, but he speaks though the spirit." The unspiritual part within this person, the soulish intellect, is not able to grasp this contemplative state. Illness has no part to play in the reason for this dark night of the purification of the desires. We have to make a choice to let go of sensual pleasures, which would usurp spiritual things by giving place to our carnal nature, and instead meditate on God's word. Sometimes the dryness lessens and one can meditate. This dark night weans the Christian from the unspiritual as God desires to humble these souls and release them from "spiritual gluttony" to "turn to spiritual things".

The Beginnings of the Dark Night of the Spirit

This soul who has gone through trials, and spiritual dryness with the purification of the senses under God's humbling hand in dealing with his spiritual gluttony, in the dark night of the soul, may now face the dark night of the spirit. However, he may still have periods of dryness for the "soul is not yet completely purified".

Not all souls go through the dark night of the spirit. As to the timing of this dark night of the spirit and who enters into the terror of this night, God is sovereign and nobody knows who or why some go through it and others are not led on this path.

An indication that the dark night of the spirit is happening is the intensifying of trials and a deeper darkness. This soul returns to its state of less spiritual dryness after his time of temptation.

> My experience in travelling through my dark night of the spirit was where I encountered evil entities attacking my mind with satanic oppression. Through these horrific encounters I believe God's purpose was my perception of a deeper outworking of His ways and acts in my life, which were higher than my feeble thoughts, when I attempted to analyse these devilish encounters. I would become totally dependent upon God and His grace, travelling this new spiritual path, and full of anguish, when it did not make sense to my intellect, my emotions or my spirit.
>
> Despite this dark night, God's refining fire was still at work, although the presence of God was absent and the presence of evil strong. God knew what He was honing in me when He was silent, and my spirit which once witnessed with God's Spirit I was His child, now felt a death in my senses.

The carnal nature within a man questions this dark night when it is so painful to go through. He does not understand why God is permitting it, or His purpose allowing his soul and spirit to know such torment and anguish! Job was a righteous man who journeyed through this dark night.

The flesh nature will never comprehend the way God leads a man, for it cannot discern the spiritual; only the witness of the spirit in the believer is able to discern the things of the Spirit through the spiritual rebirth, which is the new creation in Christ (2.Cor.5:17). The intellect is of no benefit.

Even more painful is this believer's knowledge that his help "comes from the Lord who made heaven and earth" (Ps.121:2). When he experiences satanic oppression, he endures it, for it looms as an unsurmountable brick wall, inhibiting his progress to rise in faith and stand on the promises of God, so beneficial for his edification and comfort.

This, for me, was a different road to putting off the old man (Eph.4:22) and putting on the new man (Eph.4:24), and being renewed in the spirit of my mind (Eph.4:23). This was a spiritual road I knew personally many did not travel. The aloneness of this path, the spirit within once quickened and from which I had fallen from such a height, this was part of the soul's deeper identification with Calvary.

Looking back on those past decades I can understand that through the years Christ has honed me and I possess the wisdom to love Him and others with Christ's love more richly than previously before entering the dark night of the spirit. The hellish manifestations of evil have been used by the Holy Spirit for my spiritual growth, and ultimately for my good (Rom.8:28). I did not recognise this travelling through the dark night of the spirit.

> *I will give thee the treasures of darkness, and hidden riches of secret places, that thou mayest know that I, the Lord which calleth thee by thy name am the God of Israel.*
>
> Isaiah 45:3 (KJV)

A profound work of the Holy Spirit in the flesh happens when it is crucified in this dark night, yet this believer does not experience expressions of joy or revelations to comfort and lighten his spiritual load. Characteristic of this dark night is a distinct lack of faith in God, which is painful to bear.

I remember my experience of the dark night of the spirit. It is of significance that I recall my inability journeying through this dark night to recall spiritual revelations and Bible verses which would have comforted me through this hellish experience. This is because it is part of the weaning process in the soul area from self-gratification; any past self-gratification enjoyed in one's soul area with bliss in the senses – when the soul encountered revelations, visions, fasts – is now purified in the dark night of the spirit, yet all the soul feels is an emptiness.

The senses and emotions appear to be deadened travelling through the dark night of the spirit, with the weaning off spiritual gratifications which the Christian has delighted himself in thus far through fasts and spiritual greediness, where spiritual delights brought pride, comfort, and self-importance in his soul. He now comes to see there was an element of the soulish operating in these spiritual delights, hence the spiritual dryness he feels now in his spirit, as God allows his spirit to be dormant, resting, whilst God refines his soul, and where the Christian thought he was spiritual. They were spiritual encounters with God, when he was operating through the unction of the Holy Spirit, but often the soulish operated, and so now a deeper purification is at work. This is why the dark night of the spirit is so painful, and a barren and bleak experience.

I now perceive God takes a soul along this obscure spiritual path, where no glimmer of God's light exists, where a sanctification process is nevertheless occurring and yet is often unbeknown to the soul journeying it.

This soul tastes a minute fragment of the spiritual anguish Jesus knew on the Cross, when Jesus was separated from His Father's love and bore the weight of sinful mankind. This soul is identifying with Jesus' anguish on Calvary in a more profound way, unlike how they previously encountered in their past sufferings and lofty spiritual encounters.

As one feels the loss of a love relationship with Jesus, the soul is experiencing a little of the despair Jesus knew when he was separated from His Father on the Cross of Calvary. It is as if the wounded spirit within this Christian has fallen and now exists in a death-like experience in his spirit within him, who once loved and enjoyed sweet communion with his God. This was my experience.

The soul journeying this dark night does not have a knowledge in his spirit that God is sovereign and present in his dark night and in everything that is happening in his life, neither has he the perception that God is overseeing what is being birthed in his spirit in the dark night.

At present all this soul can acknowledge inside of himself is the pain of losing Jesus as his companion, and the lack of revelation of the person of Christ within his spirit. Often Satan attacks his thought life with frightening visions and with a condemning voice, and the body may be attacked with physical ailments.

> Prayer did not shift the black dungeon of satanic oppression in the dark night, for me. This dark night is unlike the stages of spiritual growth you will have read about in previous chapters in this book. I felt treasures in darkness were concealed to me for a long while. I was naïve regarding how to grasp truth from the Bible because the darkness obscured any glimmer of light to receive revelation in my spirit, and yet I knew God's truth must be available to me. I just did not know how to find it.
>
> The agony for me journeying through my dark night of the spirit was in not having a spiritual adviser who could enlighten and guide me through it. When I attempted to explain my dilemma to believers I was reprimanded and told in no uncertain terms that I was disobedient to God and this was why I was suffering in this extraordinary way.
>
> I have come to understand decades after the event how these Christians were answering my questions from their limited spiritual perspective and judging me from their experiences and opinion that Christians only have trials if they have been disobedient to God! These

same Christians said that my dark night was God punishing me with His correction.

Dark Night Experiences

We read in the book of Job that Job was a righteous man and yet God allowed Satan to buffet him. Our trials and temptations do not denote we have a lack of sincerity or obedience in our Christian walk. We may be journeying through their dark night of the soul or spirit.

St John talks of the necessity for a believer to obtain a spiritual adviser who can enlighten him on his path travelling the dark night.

> *This is the moment when souls turn back if they do not find somebody who understands them, to be their guide; they leave the road, become dispirited or at least they are prevented from making further progress because of the great effort they find in trying to advance along the road of reasoning and meditation. They tire themselves out because they imagine that they are failing because of their own negligence and sin. But all their efforts are in vain because God is taking them down another road, the road of contemplation, which is so different from the first road. One belongs to meditation and human intellect while the other has nothing to do with meditation and human intellect.*

The despair in the believer who has walked closely with God, appears more apparent with an inability to comprehend this spiritual dark road of terror. The loneliness of this path is made more painful when Christians naïvely fail to recognise how or why a person is in this spiritual plight, on observing their spiritual walk shows evidence of a close relationship with God.

Oh, the isolation of this spiritual dark night! I could not articulate to anyone this spiritual night of the wounded spirit when I journeyed through it. It was often too painful a dark night to share.

The wounded spirit dwells in deep despair and is unable to take away from this road any enlightenment or comfort. It is a road on which he rationalises that God has unwittingly thrust the dark night of the spirit upon him. There is no comfort or solace in this dark night, which is unlike previous spiritual roads the Christian has travelled. The soul and spirit travels through total blackness.

Arguably, the spiritual paths I have written about in the previous chapters of this book appear trivial in comparison to that journeyed by the soul with a wounded spirit passing through the dark night; and yet the truth remains that every spiritual stage is of vital importance for a Christian's spiritual growth. This soul will find this truth hard to grasp in the dark night of the soul.

The dark night of the spirit is a unique spiritual path, and not comparable to the times when God withdraws His presence so that the child of God will learn to rely on His word and not on feelings of His presence. It also differs to the spiritual road of the Lord's chastening and the pain when God strips away fleshly desires and reveals to us our selfish motives. This is a painful dark night in itself!

The characteristics of the wounded spirit in this dark night is a loneliness of one's self cut off from the Lover. This soul is often misunderstood and their reputation slandered through ignorance and lack of spiritual discernment of the purifying process God is accomplishing through the dark night.

This dark night is different to that of temptation, which all Christians face, for it is when we are tempted that we go to Jesus for succour and strength to aid us in the trial.

Regardless of the negative emotions, Christians who travel through this dark night may acknowledge in their emotions that God is nevertheless quickening their spirit within them. The wounded spirit at this stage in the dark night of the spirit feels a lifelessness and deadening. He is bereft of a quickening in the emotions towards God or the people he meets. This Christian comes to acknowledge eventually that this unusual dark night has been ordained by God for him.

The emotions still remain dormant, whilst the spirit within often does not bear witness that he has been born again of the Spirit of God, although buried deep in his emotions he knows he has. This is part of the horror of this dark night.

As if this is not enough, the soul suffers the fiery darts of satanic oppression. Confused by evil entities harassing the thought life, he finds himself powerless to pray. At church, if this soul can stay inside its walls, he may not join in effortlessly with singing the spiritual songs. At times, his vocal cords may restrict, as though invisible hands were restricting his breathing. He may have frightening satanic visions which make him afraid to pray. He may hear Satan condemning him in his thoughts. I experienced all these things in journeying though the dark night of the spirit.

This soul who is able to hear God speak amidst the confusion of satanic oppression, can say, like Job, "I have heard of thee by the hearing of the ear, but now mine eye seeth thee." (Job.42:5, KJV).

The believer may echo these words in his spirit if he can hear the wisdom of God speaking to him amidst the confusion in this dark night. It often takes a long while and sometimes even years in this dark night of the wounded spirit, before a person can grasp any light of revelation from God as to the meaning of this season and God's intentions in bringing purpose to his life.

This Christian's spirit has been wounded. "The spirit of a man sustaineth his infirmity, but a wounded spirit who can bear?" (Prov.8:14, KJV). The wounded spirit is aching within himself to reach out to God for help during the frightening satanic oppression he is enduring, and the despairing numbness which has now become his only reality in his senses. Satan's fiery darts have pierced his spirit. The agony of separation from God is unbearable; it is real, and a lonely road for this soul to bear, not least because the presence of evil is so real to him.

This soul is bereft in thinking he has forever lost his love relationship with God, but because this dark night has been tailored by God for His purposes to be fulfilled in his life, he must endure this road!

Of course, the flesh does not want to endure! It is in danger of rising in anger and blaming God, like Job's wife who said to him, "Do you still remain your integrity? Curse God and die." (Job.2:9, KJV). Likewise, the person travelling through the dark night of the spirit is tempted to curse God as to why He should allow him to fall into such a dark pit.

> When I experienced a wounded spirit in this dark night, I faced the same dilemma: whether to rebel and to curse God, or to trust Him in the dark. The correct attitude would have been to embrace this unknown path of pain in my faculties. I could not bear the pain in my soul in missing Jesus as a reality in my life. I knew a little of the fellowship of His sufferings now, but I still struggled to understand that this path was planned by God.
>
> After a year and a half had elapsed in the dark night of the spirit, the satanic oppression caused a weakness in my soul, spirit, and body. I had lost the will to fight against the spirits of wickedness. I did not understand that there would come a time where this dry spiritual

experience would reap its contemplative treasures. I had to travel many years in this dark night, and many more still, before God revealed Himself to me and I was ready to receive the blessings of the treasures of darkness that were available to me. Decades later I am still receiving through a divine revelation in my spirit the treasures in darkness, as I walk with Him.

St John explains how the soul in the dry spells does not "take pleasure in its dry state, which comes from the purification of the physical senses". There is, however, spiritual food to be had with which he may nourish himself, which is "the inner food" of contemplation. "It is both dark and dry to the senses."

Unfortunately, when God was in the process of leading me along this obscure path of the dark night of the spirit, I did not know any spiritual advisors advanced in their spiritual walk who would comprehend this path and instruct me with spiritual guidance and wisdom. At this period in my Christian walk I was not able to reach this contemplative spiritual state God desired. In my ignorance, listening to Satan's lies that God had abandoned me to suffer, I rebelled against God. I fell foul of Satan's arrows penetrating the depths of my soul and spirit.

I rebelled in anger against God and the dark night of the spirit. I could not face the loneliness, the emptiness inside my soul and the mental struggle of praying against evil entities which oppressed my thought life.

If I had been able to muster a grain of faith like a mustard seed within myself me to fight the onslaughts of Satan, maybe I would not have rebelled against God, but I did not possess the mental strength to rise in faith or the spiritual muscle to fight the spiritual darkness in this dark night.

God has restored to me "the years that the locust have eaten", and I now have a testimony to share to encourage others journeying their dark night of the spirit. All things work together for good.

By night I sought Him whom my soul loveth: I sought Him: but I found Him not.

Song of Solomon 3:1 (KJV)

The Dark Nights of the Soul and the Spirit

The wounded spirit in this dark night misses his Saviour, for he remembers he once shared a love song with his God. Now this soul cannot find God and has lost his song in the dark night of the spirit.

The dilemma for this soul is whether he chooses to rebel against God, knowing Satan will leave him alone if he walks carnally, or to say in the face of the devil, "Though He slay me, yet will I trust Him." (Job.13:15).

When a believer reaches the crossroads in this spiritual stage there occurs a quickening in their spirit in recognising God's sanctifying work within them. In God's time the "treasures in darkness" will be revealed (Is.45:3). This soul will once more arise out of the ashes, but for now his spirit must lay dormant whilst the painful purifying process continues.

Chapter Eleven

The Quest for Spiritual Enlightenment

THIS SOUL IS QUICKENED AND IS NOW AWARE OF A DEEEPER richness in his spirit through journeying through the dark night of the spirit. The truth has never been so real that, "Without Him I can do nothing." He knows this wholeheartedly and with a greater measure than in all his past temptations and trials.

The soul's exploration through the dark night means he is often unable to worship God with the same intensity as before he entered the dark night and lacks the spiritual strength to engage in spiritual warfare against the enemy.

He laments what he presumes he has permanently lost spiritually, his love relationship with Jesus. We have already explored how this soul faces a dilemma whether to rebel against God or cling onto God's faithfulness in the dark, when it appears Satan has the upper hand.

When looking into the life of Job, we find there was no man to be found in the land as righteous as Job (Job.1:8). Nevertheless, Job questioned God when faced with disaster. His friends did not help him. They pointed the finger and criticised him regarding the disasters which had befallen him. They unwisely claimed he had acted unrighteously against his God by displeasing Him, and therefore Job deserved the adversity which had overtaken him. Job's friends were insistent in blaming him for his demise.

At the end of the narrative, Job hears God speaking to him in his distress.

> Then the Lord answered Job out of the whirlwind and said: Who is this that darkens counsel by words without knowledge? Gird up thy loins like a man; I will demand of thee, and answer thou me.
>
> *Job 38:1-3 (KJV)*

The Quest for Spiritual Enlightenment

Job now knows he misunderstood God. His spiritual eyes are opened, and he acknowledges God is sovereign over every catastrophe that has befallen him in his adversity. God is not to be questioned in His dealings with mankind. Job was a righteous man, and yet in his distress he questioned why God would allow such adversity in the loss of his livelihood, family, and health.

Eventually, God turns Job's self-pity and his questions into knowledge and so Job gains spiritual understanding when he listens to the wisdom of God. He now *knows* God is sovereign over everything that has happened in his life.

> *I have heard of thee by the hearing of the ear but now my eye seeth thee.*
>
> Job 42:5 (KJV)

Job had heard about God; he was familiar with hearing God's voice and he was obedient to Him. He was a righteous man who lived a life pleasing to God, but when his loss was so grievous and his health suffered, his friends deserted him, and he lost his family, he cursed God and the day he was born. In effect he lost the will to live.

Eventually he made an end of listening to his friends' unwise counsel and instead listened to the wisdom of God to him in the dark night. It was while Job listened to God that he received revelation from God and exclaimed, "But now my eye sees you." (Job.42:5).

Job knew the acts of God, but now he saw the adversity he suffered with new spiritual eyes and he came to understand his circumstances from God's viewpoint and not from the viewpoint of his friends' limited wisdom and counsel.

Job's spiritual eyes were opened when God confronted him and he acknowledged more fully God's infinite wisdom in His dealings with mankind, which he now knew to be higher than man's wisdom. He repented before his God when he heard Him confront him on all that had befallen him. God spoke with wisdom when he challenged Job's dialogue surrounding his calamity.

Job's example of suffering helps us to evaluate our own suffering not from our own perspective, but from knowing that God is sovereign and that He has a plan for our lives already mapped out.

The Soul's Quest in the Dark Night

What is the soul's quest for spiritual enlightenment in this dark night of the spirit? To answer this question, we must delve into the Song of Solomon where the symbolic love relationship between the Lover and the Beloved can be used as a metaphor of Jesus and the Church.

> *Behold you are beautiful my love your eyes are doves, behold you are beautiful, my Beloved, truly lovely.*
>
> Song of Solomon 1:15,16 (KJV)

The soul has worshipped the beauty he has seen in his Lover. He has known an intimate and tender relationship with his God. He has experience this first hand. He has adored the tenderness in his Lover's eyes, which has cemented a loyal love between them.

This dark night affects this soul who has travelled on a quest in search of his Lover, which is Jesus.

> *I will rise me now, and go about the city in the streets, and in the broad ways I will seek Him whom my soul loveth. I sought Him but I found Him not.*
>
> Song of Solomon 3:2

This is a painful journey for this soul in the dark night, for he does not know why he is in darkness, or why he cannot find his Lover. He prays fervently, seeking God's presence in the darkness, but cannot find any peace of mind. He may repent of all known sin, but he remains in darkness.

This soul may wander into churches and asks his fellow Christians, have you seen my Lord?

> *The watchmen who go about the city found me;*
> *I said, "Have you seen the one I love?"*
>
> Song of Solomon 3:3 (KJV)

If they have seen the Lover, why cannot the soul in the dark night find Him?

This soul in the dark night questions his friends' advice, just as Job questioned his friends. This dark night is an obscure road to the nominal Christian and there would seem no justification as to why the soul is shrouded in this dark and lonely night. The anguished soul does not realise this is part of God's plan, the isolation and loneliness of this spiritual road so unfamiliar to any road he has trod before. Along this road this soul identifies with Jesus and His sufferings on the Cross with a profoundness previously unknown in his Christian experience. God will create a purification in his soul from a greedy spirit and desires for spiritual things to bless his soul, which could not be accomplished in the putting off the deeds of the flesh alone.

If only this soul could grasp this truth! Journeying through this purifying process he finds he has not yet received revelation from God as to why this dark night is happening to him. He must travel this road by faith. Faith is hard for this soul to find because often a black cloak of depression and satanic oppression accompanies this dark night, which further confuses and hinders his spiritual discernment.

For a while, the Father turned His back on the Son of God, on Calvary's Cross, and likewise this soul, in identifying with Jesus' anguish on the Cross, discovers a little of this darkness and loneliness in his separation from Jesus. This soul is identifying with Jesus in His darkest hour. He feels he is shrouded in a black pit of darkness and has truly been crucified to his fleshly deeds in the dark night of the wounded spirit.

> This was my experience when I journeyed through my dark night. I attended Christian conferences hoping to obtain an answer and insight into my horrific encounter with darkness, but I did not receive it. At one time during this prolonged dark night the angel of death stood by my bed at night strangling me to kill me! I managed to speak in the heavenly language God had given me (in tongues) and the devil retreated (1.Cor.12).

There is a tendency for this soul in the dark night to cling to what is familiar to him and which he has spiritually learnt in the past, for this has been his security before in trials. This soul is obedient to God in adopting biblical principles and has faith in the promises of God. His intentions are to be close to God, and so he repents of his sin whilst continuing to question God why he is on this indistinct spiritual path.

Unfortunately, he is apt to fail in his quest to find answers to his questions because he is looking in the wrong places for solace, but does not recognise this. Some believers in the dark night of the spirit will omit asking God to purify them through the dark night, most probably because this dark night of the spirit is alien to them, and they struggle to comprehend what has happened to their wounded spirit.

This soul's resolve is to discover a way out of the dark night, which he views like a maze, but this quest only hinders him from learning God's purpose in it. The reason for this dullness in his spiritual faculties is that this spiritual dark night is so painful to the senses, his spirit, and his body. Often evil spirits torment the thoughts. There are usually no spiritual advisors around equipped to enlighten him on this path, and like the children of Israel he may grumble in his wilderness state.

Usually a lack of discernment exists within this soul as to why this dark night is happening and ultimately what this path is meant to teach him. There is a tendency for him to let his emotions guide him through obscurity, instead of the word of God and the Holy Spirit directing him into truth to illuminate his dark road.

He is on dangerous ground in opening a door for the carnal nature to usurp the hope of hearing God's voice in the darkness, amidst his confusing and conflicting thoughts. He may have unlocked his heart to a bitter spirit in conversation with God and when in possession of a bitter spirit, God's purification is momentarily halted. Unless this soul acknowledges his plight, God is unable to guide him into the purification of the senses. God waits on this soul to be rid of a bitter spirit before He can instruct him.

This soul may be angry at God and so his bitter spirit separates him further from his Lover. The carnal nature must choose to die to questions, doubts, self-pity, and bitterness. This soul has enslaved himself and is in grave danger of being trapped in further bondage by the devil.

If only this soul could understand, "My thoughts are not your thoughts, and my ways are higher than your ways," (Is.55:8,9, KJV) he would find comfort for his soul.

For now, God watches over his child, waiting patiently for him to submit his will to God's. All is dead in this soul's emotions and a wounded spirit which once knew the glory of God is now pining its loss. Every part of him aches for God's deliverance.

He Feedeth Among the Lilies

We find a rejoicing in the union between the Lover and the soul, whose longing in the dark night of the soul is to be reunited with his Lover. Jesus goes into the garden of his soul and "He feedeth amongst the lilies" (Song.2:16, KJV).

The Lover is rejoicing in the fruits of the Holy Spirit which He has cultivated within this Christian's soul and which have remained so long dormant in the dark night.

It is now that this soul knows to a greater degree that "without God, he can do nothing", more than any spiritual road could teach him and upon which God has previously led him. He has clung on feebly to God in his spiritual blackness and despair, and having nursed a wounded spirit for so long, this believer is now beginning to understand God's ways with new spiritual eyes, as Job did.

The soul begins to rejoice in the dark night, because his spiritual ears hear his Lover calling through the lattice of the window, even though his spirit still largely dwells in darkness. He awakens to the knowledge that the hand of God *was* present throughout the dark night! This soul is gently wooed by his Lover and on hearing His voice, his heart responds with an ache of longing for the Lover with an exquisite yet bittersweet joy.

> *Awake O north wind and come thou south; blow upon my garden that the spices thereof may flow out. Let my beloved come into his garden and eat of his pleasant fruits.*
>
> Song of Solomon 4:16 (KJV)

This verse is a metaphor of the blowing wind of the Holy Spirit upon the garden of the soul, which is being sanctified in this dark night and is now bestowed with the fruits of the Holy Spirit.

> *But the fruit of the spirit is love, joy, peace, patience, kindness, self-control; against such there is no law. And those who belong to Christ have crucified the flesh with its passions and desires.*
>
> Galatians 5:22:23,24

> *Let my beloved come into his garden and eat the pleasant fruits.*
>
> Song of Solomon 4:16

This is what Jesus does. His delight is to eat of the graces and fruits which He has created through the Holy Spirit in the soul, and He rejoices over the sanctification process in the garden of the soul, which He has cultivated.

Oh, let those spices spread their fragrance born in the dark night of the spirit. Oh, that the scent of the spices would flow out to those we meet who are hurting, who are without hope in this world. Who better to do this than the soul who has borne with grace and persevered in the dark night of the soul with a wounded spirit?

Maybe like me you have resisted the dark night's instruction through a distinct lack of spiritual advisors along its road. Nevertheless, in the end we emerge from the darkness with a deeper revelation of God than before embarking upon this road. God is merciful and full of grace.

The Quickening Power of the Holy Spirit

The spirit long lay dormant within this Christian but now he receives a quickening in his spirit. For a fleeting moment he experiences that he is not alone. He has a glimpse of his Lover, He whom his soul loves. This glimpse enlivens his deadened spirit. This spiritual awakening is bittersweet, because his wounded spirit is still a reminder of Jesus whom he loves and whom he has presumed lost forever, feeling abandoned by God.

Negative emotions are apt to rise and are compounded by an unforgiving spirit towards the Lover for the torment this soul has undergone in the dark night and his separation from sweet communion with Jesus; until now with this glimpse of his Lover.

This soul looks through the lattice and his soul leaps within for his Lover. He cannot contain his joy, so long has his spirit lain dormant in the dark night without a knowledge of God's love in his faculties.

> *My beloved was like a roe or a young heart: behold He standeth behind a wall; he looketh forth at the windows shewing Himself through the lattice.*
>
> Song of Solomon 2:9

The soul is overjoyed at this fleeting revelation of Jesus in his spirit and his emotions leap for joy! Long has his soul and spirit been in the dark night where spiritual feasts were nowhere to be found.

Participating in worldly pleasurers and turning a back on God would dishonour God, though surely it would bring transient relief to the believer in the dark night? The soul is in torment and despair when he thinks on these things, yet he is grateful God would consider him a mere

The Quest for Spiritual Enlightenment

mortal! He is beginning in the dark night to love Jesus for who He is and not require any blessing or token of spiritual things from Him.

This soul is now content just to look through the lattice at his Saviour. It brings exquisite joy to his spirit. It is a treasure in his darkness.

More enjoyable with his glimpse of God is the change within his deadened soul. He has endured the dark night and now gently trickling into his spirit is a token of God's love, whilst he largely remains in his spiritual night.

It differs to previous glimpses of God, where His presence was strong in carrying his soul through many an adverse circumstance. This soul is beginning to experience treasures in darkness, flashes of light, and holiness becoming clear to his spiritual vision.

This soul knows that all past revelation, visions, wisdom, even how God had used Him in the past for His kingdom, was all because of God's grace. He now understands the benefit of the road of contemplation as opposed to the meditative state which he journeyed through as a spiritual beginner.

In the silence of the dark night of obscurity in soul and spirit, with a deep depression, satanic oppression and rejection from spiritual advisers, a sanctifying work by the Lover in the darkest place of the purification of the senses and in his spirit has occurred. It has taken this dark night of the soul to comprehend it, when all the soul has experienced is darkness in the faculties.

This soul has no strength left to praise God, and no strength to overcome satanic oppression. Any glimpse of God, any movement of the Lover towards this soul, it all had to come from God! There is deep joy in this soul at this stage of his spiritual journey.

This soul now remembers how he perceived himself spiritually mature when he remembers his giftings and past revelations from God! He now comes to an understanding of his immaturity in not discerning the ways of God with man.

This soul's reputation may be in tatters, ostracised by those who criticise him in thinking unwisely God is punishing him for his sin. This soul in the dark night will come to see that God often uses a reputation which has been slandered unfairly to deal with the pride within him.

Spying his Lover though the lattice, is a treasure in his darkness during this spiritual isolation and misunderstanding from others. All has appeared dead in his spiritual walk, yet unbeknown to him at this stage in the dark night, God's sanctifying process is at work within his spirit.

It is unlike any past revelation he has received from God in his Christian walk. Now it brings enough joy just to glimpse his Lover through the lattice.

Written below is Neil Perry's experience and account of the dark night of the soul.

Neil Perry's Experience of the Dark Night of the Soul

> I became a Christian in 1976, and I was baptised in the Holy Spirit a few weeks later. At this point in my life I had a simple, almost childlike faith, trusting Christ in all things.
>
> My spiritual understanding grew as I studied God's word. I found the love of God to be all-compassing as I prayed for guidance. The Church became my family with my fellow brother and sisters in Christ. I was full of Jesus and the Holy Spirit and felt a need in my heart to reach out to non-believers and tell them about the Saviour.
>
> A few months passed and I didn't feel so close to the Lord. I became worried, fearing I may have upset God. It was during this period I found myself in the midst of temptation, which became a constant battle for me. On some occasions I lost the battle against temptation and I took it badly, fearing I had betrayed the Lord's trust He had in me.
>
> I was attending many Christian meetings, reading spiritual books, but was neglecting God's word and prayer. This happened gradually.
>
> Around the same time, I was baptised in water at my local church. Soon after my baptism a woman at the church asked me how I felt. I replied that I felt alright. This mature woman of God explained to me that after being baptised in water I was to expect the attacks of the devil which would test my faith. I thought I could withstand anything!
>
> A few weeks later, it felt as though all of hell had broken loose. One night in bed I felt an evil mocking spirit fill my room. The atmosphere appeared murky with a musty aroma. The mocking spirit was instructing me to blaspheme against Christ and the Holy Spirit. I was sweating with fear and continuously repeating the name Jesus. I could almost make out the sound of chains rattling as I cowered in my room. I was feeling lost and it made me feel worse when I recalled the scripture verse, "There is no fear in love, perfect love casts out fear." (1.Jn.4:18). I was a new Christian and thought that since I was fearful, I must have failed Christ.

The next morning, I tried to forget everything that happened that night and decided maybe I was taking my faith too seriously. This led me to hang out with my old non-Christian friends because fighting this spiritual battle was too much for me to handle.

In my experience I believe I came under attack from the devil as I was over-spiritualising my faith by not relying on the Lord with a simple, trusting faith anymore. When the Lord died on the Cross He said, "It is finished." (Jn.19:30). Somehow, I had slipped into trying to live by the law rather than trusting Christ who had fulfilled everything.

All Jesus wants from us is to love and to please Him, not by works, but by being grateful for what He did for us; His ministry, death on the Cross, and rising from the dead into life, to bring us to the Father.

Epilogue

I WANT TO DANCE ON HIGH PLACES! I DESIRE MY SPIRITUAL roots to be firmly planted in the soil, and have my feet standing on the Rock, Christ Jesus. He alone is the firm foundation for all Christians.

Where are you in your walk with God? We are all want to grow in our faith. Temptations and trials will come to us whether we have walked the Christian road for many years or are starting the journey with God. Trials and temptations come to the novice believer, the spiritually weak, and the mature believer.

The baptism in the Holy Spirit which the early Church received, empowered them with boldness to share the gospel. It was a boldness they did not possess in the natural.

> *...preaching the Kingdom of God, and teaching those things which concern the Lord Jesus Christ, with all confidence, no man forbidding him.*
>
> Acts 28:31

Jesus bestows the gifts of the Spirit following the baptism in the Holy Spirit. These gifts Jesus is only too willing to give to the Church to bring it encouragement and blessing. The baptism in the Holy Spirit empowers a Christian to walk with God in holiness.

What you have read within these pages has been a long journey for me these past forty-eight years as a Christian. I have known glory times with Jesus, and the darkest night of the soul imaginable, with satanic oppression and depression.

Am I still standing? Yes, of course! The teaching within these pages is the outworking of my faith in God over many decades, which I have personally experienced and learnt from the Bible as I have sat at the feet of Jesus, who is my greatest teacher.

Along my Christian journey Jesus has guided, corrected, and taught me through the Bible and by divine revelation in my spirit. The longer I walk with Him the more I recognise how much there is to learn about Him, and to experience the fullness of the Holy Spirit in quickening me in my spirit and purifying me to be like my Saviour. Oh, how much I want my life to reflect my Saviour!

Epilogue

You reach a stage in your progress with God when you realise there is so much more to experience of Jesus, in reaching the full stature of wisdom and revelation of God, and which God longs to outwork spiritually in the Christian who trusts and obeys Him. We will never reach full maturity in our walk with God until we meet Him in glory!

Long gone are the days when, as a young Christian experiencing visions and the gifts of the Holy Spirit, I thought I was mature in my faith, measuring myself against those who had not received such gifts and blessings!

Oh, how immature I was and naïve in the way God works in His dealings with His children. How full of pride! The stripping away process of the carnal nature has been a painful process for me.

In conclusion, what have I learnt along my journey?

Firstly, I have a deeper empathy and understanding when I see fellow Christians weak in their faith, perhaps finding the Christian road an arduous journey. I see the road from God's perspective now, having been through the dark night of the soul. I do not blame people for their backslidings. Sometimes the cross we bear is so painful that walking away from His Cross seems an easier option. Some people are oppressed by Satan, or in deep depression. There are many reasons for Christians to backslide. I am very aware of my past, and how I backslid from God in my dark nights of the soul and spirit. Who am I to judge others?

Secondly, I understand other people more fully going through their own trial of their faith, and temptations. I can help them understand this path from the Bible's perspective. I can sit where they sit because I have been in the place where my trials have overwhelmed me and the temptation to sin was so great that I succumbed to its power. I would have loved a helping hand in those days. The dark night of the spirit has created compassion within me more than on the mountaintop experience and my glory days of the richest blessings. I used to think, before my plunge into the dark night of the spirit, that Christians were not as desirous of a deep commitment to God as I was, and that was why they were not blessed by God as I had been! How immature I was in my faith in those early days! How full of pride, which I did not see in myself back then.

Thirdly, we are regenerated by the new birth through the blood of Jesus shed on the Cross. The human nature is naturally and intrinsically selfish. We operate out of our carnal nature before we are regenerated and born again of the Spirit of God. After we become Christians through the spiritual new birth, we still have the old deeds of the flesh nature which tries to dominate us in ruling our thoughts, emotions, and actions. I understand the tug of war between the carnal nature and the new nature, having matured and learnt the ways of God over the past decades, through suffering and by God's correction. The Christian faith is not only about miracles, healings, the gifts of the Holy Spirit, and being blessed by God! It is not only experiencing His acts, as amazing as they are. It is about God making us fit vessels for His use, to lead people to Christ, to bring a harvest full of souls into the kingdom of God. We must be honed as a precious jewel, Jesus cutting off our rough edges to create us into fit vessels for Him to use in His kingdom work.

Fourthly, I have learnt what matters to God is what He produces within our soul, the fruits of the Holy Spirit. He wants us to be pure, fervent, and authentic witnesses as Christians who bear His name.

Through the stages of spiritual development – His correction; the withdrawal of His presence, which teaches us to love Him for who He is and not merely for His presence and blessings; through our trials and temptations; learning to die to self; equipping us to be spiritual warriors through an intercessory prayer life; and the dark nights of the soul and the spirit – God wants to lead all Christians into maturity of faith. This maturing process sanctifies and equips us for service. We in turn give God the glory for what He has wrought within us by the power of the Holy Spirit. God wants all Christians to become effective witnesses in bearing fruit in the saving of precious souls.

Dancing with the devil is not an option. I danced with the devil in my dark night of the soul after years of struggling spiritually against satanic oppression, and because I could not cope with the spiritual darkness in my dark night of the spirit. I thought the dark night of the spirit had cost me the most precious person I have known: my Jesus. My dark night did not take Jesus by surprise! Jesus knew this road He had planned for me and it would be yet another stage in my spiritual growth. He was leading me along a rocky road and one with many twists and turns but it would bring me to maturity in Him. I am still learning and growing after more than forty years in my journey with God.

Joshua said, "...choose this day whom you will serve..." (Josh.24:15). The best advice is to serve and love God with all your heart. Be faithful to Him through the different paths He will lead you along, and when the road gets rocky remember God's desire is to purify you

Epilogue

through the varying stages of spiritual development and growth which you will encounter.

Stay faithful to Him no matter how tough the road ahead. Remain faithful even in the dark night of the spirit, which some of you will travel as I have. You will find exquisite treasures in darkness. Even the rocky roads exist to ultimately bless you.

Go God's way and not your own. The Christian walk does not consist of how much God blesses us, but rather how we may please and bless God and others through a life of obedience to Him.

Let Satan have a pity party! God can turn the darkest night, the greatest suffering, our temptations and trials, and yes, even the darkest nights of the soul and spirit into our greatest triumphs; and at the end of life's journey an eternity is waiting for us to be spent in heaven with Jesus.

This is surely the greatest reason to rise as spiritual warriors: because the alternative, if we do not know Christ, is too awful to imagine; it is an eternity without Jesus lived in hell (Rom.6:23).

Do you know Jesus? He is calling you now.

...we are more than conquerors through Christ who loved us.
Romans 8:37

Forgiven, cleansed, justified, corrected, and sanctified. It is time to go into the world and share what God has done for *you!*

You are God's chosen warrior!

You are not a victim of your circumstance. If you know Him, you are a restored child of God. Satan is under your feet and you walk on the spiritual heights.

Walk in the freedom of the Cross!

He sets me on my high places.
Psalm 18:33

Also by the Author

Darkness to Destiny
ISBN: 978-1-911086-67-3
Published by Onwards and Upwards

A boarding school for girls was radically transformed when one of the pupils encountered Jesus and began to share her newfound faith. Gwynneth was one of the first to follow in devoting her life to Christ, and the revival that followed had far-reaching effects.

Gwynneth completed her education, not with great academic qualifications, but with a calling from heaven to reach out to the homeless and rejected with the love of Jesus. She invested herself in spending time with, and praying for, the marginalised, but her efforts soon led to burnout, followed by a rapid downward spiral emotionally and spiritually. She began to encounter satanic activity, depression and sickness, along with abuse and rejection from those around her. At times she made poor choices. Gradually she found herself drawn into the world of drug addiction, with poverty, suffering and violence.

God seemed distant and Gwynneth found herself trapped beyond her ability to escape. But she could not forget her childhood encounter with Jesus. In the midst of great darkness, she clung on to the hope of her destiny.

Available from your local Christian bookshop or from the publisher:
www.onwardsandupwards.org/**darkness-to-destiny**